D0853065

Between
LIFE
and
DEATH

ADVANCE PRAISE FOR THE BOOK

'Finally, finally a book—Dr Kashyap's *Between Life and Death*—that takes us through the keyhole of an intimately personal experience—the death of a loved one. From personal experience, I can tell you that the book acted as an overseer and then became a personal guide, a confidante, and an offer of hope and dignity through a period of immense suffering. I highly recommend this book wherever it goes'—Raell Padamsee, managing director, ACE Productions and Numero Uno Productions

'I have come to know Dr Kashyap Patel over the years and can honestly say there is no better spirit. He has dedicated his life to doing good for all the humanity he comes in contact with. This book is a tribute to that honesty, humanity, compassion and dedication to his patients, his colleagues and his family. This truly permeates his life in all the best ways'—Dr Ralph Boccia, chief medical officer, International Oncology Network, the US

'This much-feared and taboo topic—dying, in the best possible way—desperately needs addressing. I do not know anyone better than Dr Kashyap Patel to do so. His depth of medical knowledge, genuine care and concern, his comforting, supportive way, his positive attitude, his making himself so available day and night, all make him the best in this space. A highly evolved spiritual being, he has given my father a new lease of life twice over, when others had all but given up on him medically. That's ten years and counting, so far. Although no one is born who one day won't die, for this added time, I shall be ever grateful. Thank you is too small an expression. I eagerly await the launch of this book—selfishly, yes, but also selflessly, as I know one can weigh his words as gold, and that this book will be a priceless gift to millions out there'—Nawaz Modi Singhania, founder, Body Art fitness centres

'"Death is a brief pause in our journey," writes Dr Kashyap Patel, in this deep and profound examination of human fear when dealing with cancer. Written with extraordinary sensitivity and a deep understanding of our multiple anxieties, *Between Life and Death* gave me a great deal of strength to confront the inevitable'—Shobhaa De, journalist and author

Between
LIFE
and
DEATH

from despair to hope

DR KASHYAP PATEL

**EBURY
PRESS**

An imprint of Penguin Random House

EBURY PRESS

USA | Canada | UK | Ireland | Australia
New Zealand | India | South Africa | China

Ebury Press is part of the Penguin Random House group of companies
whose addresses can be found at global.penguinrandomhouse.com

Published by Penguin Random House India Pvt. Ltd
7th Floor, Infinity Tower C, DLF Cyber City,
Gurgaon 122 002, Haryana, India

Penguin
Random House
India

First published in Ebury Press by Penguin Random House India 2020

Copyright © Dr Kashyap Patel 2020

All rights reserved

10 9 8 7 6 5 4 3 2 1

The views and opinions expressed in this book are the author's own and the
facts are as reported by him which have been verified to the extent possible,
and the publishers are not in any way liable for the same.

ISBN 9780670093977

Typeset in Adobe Garamond Pro by Manipal Technologies Limited, Manipal
Printed at Replika Press Pvt. Ltd, India

This book is sold subject to the condition that it shall not, by way of trade
or otherwise, be lent, resold, hired out, or otherwise circulated without the
publisher's prior consent in any form of binding or cover other than that in
which it is published and without a similar condition including this condition
being imposed on the subsequent purchaser.

www.penguin.co.in

MIX
Paper from
responsible sources
FSC® C016779

Contents

Introduction: What Does It Mean to Die Well?   vii

1. Destination Unknown   1
2. The Cycle of Life and Death   19
3. What Is Death?   32
4. Dreams Shattered   45
5. Death, You Lost Today   91
6. How the Judeo-Christian Faith Regards Death   126
7. The Beginning of the End or the End of the Beginning?   135
8. Preparing to Soar   150
9. Many Bodies, One Soul   160
10. John's Goodbye   170
11. The Quest for Immortality   180
12. The Fourth Dimension   184
13. The Flight to Eternity   200

Epilogue: Concluding My Journey   215

Introduction

What Does It Mean to Die Well?

O teach me to see Death and not to fear,
But rather to take truce!
How often have I seen you at the bier,
And there look fresh and spruce!
You fragrant flowers! Then teach me, that my breath
Like yours may perfume and sweeten my death.

—Henry King, Bishop of Chichester

Steve Jobs once said, 'No one wants to die. Even people who want to go to heaven don't want to die to get there. And yet, death is the destination we all share. No one has ever escaped it. And that is as it should be, because death is very likely the single best invention of life. It is life's change agent. It clears out the old to make way for the new.'

Everyone understands the inevitability of death. We all know that our time is limited, and we see it around us as we go about our daily lives. We see our grandparents—and eventually, our parents—pass away from old age as we are left to mourn. We suffer the loss of friends to things no one could have predicted—a car accident or a sudden heart attack. We are acutely aware that our time on earth is limited to a finite number of ticks of the clock; indeed, we don't have any clue as to what that allotment is. We see the inevitability of death in the news when a hurricane strikes and leaves hundreds dead in its wake, or when an earthquake levels a city, along with many of the souls residing in it.

And yet, despite the omnipresence of death around us, no one ever wants to think about it, or talk about it, or prepare for it. An unspoken fear surrounds the topic, almost as if people believe that if they avoid talking about it, they might be able to stave off its strike.

Certain manifestations of death are especially singled out as harbingers of this fear. I see this every day in my professional life as a practising oncologist. The moment the words 'cancer' and 'death' are mentioned in a conversation, the listener invariably recoils in horror.

Millions of people every year experience this recoil when diagnosed with cancer, abruptly forced to face the sudden fear of impending death behind the curtain of the fatal words, 'I'm afraid you have cancer.' Their plans come to a screeching halt, and like a deer in the headlights, they are forced into a life of little more than waiting for that final breath before they pass away.

It is at that moment that the eternal awareness that we all know deep down rises to the surface—that, like everyone else, they know that they, too, will be leaving this world.

Until that moment, the desire to cling to life in an almost mythological quest for eternity, combined with often-profoundly mischaracterized illusions around the latest discoveries in science, had created a happy mirage of longevity. Until confronted with a stark eventuality, we all think we're going to live forever.

This causes us to suffer more when the shroud of an impending demise lifts. I see it every day—patients in their last few days enduring horrifically painful therapies when we have already informed them that the end result of that dreadful suffering will be maybe two or three more weeks of life spent in agonizing pain. The pain and the therapy do not allow them to spend time with their loved ones or enjoy the comforts of life. Those few weeks are spent chained to a hospital bed. We are too willing, it seems, to bargain away quality time with those we love and freedom from debilitating pain in exchange for just a few more days on earth. And in that last leg of the marathon, instead of preparing and planning for a graceful and pain-free departure surrounded by those we hold dear, we prefer to ruin those precious moments in pursuit of a far-fetched cure—ensuring that the final days we spend on earth are the most miserable of our entire lives.

It is this fate that, as a physician who has been at the deathbed of countless patients, I want to help people avoid.

Treatment has advanced to the point where we can successfully treat and cure some forms of cancer. Even when the disease is incurable, we can add years to one's life. And when there is no hope left, we have the ability to provide patients with estimates of how much time they have before the disease takes them, and give them the opportunity to plan for their exit. At that point, when therapy fails, when a timer has been placed on our moments walking the earth, the single-most important thing we can do is prepare.

When the topic comes up, the gut reaction is usually 'I don't want to die'. This is a perfectly natural and life-affirming thought, and it is true that if we constantly think about death, we lose the ability to live our lives to the fullest. But there are exceptions. When faced with the certain knowledge that death is approaching on a relatively predictable timetable, despite not wanting to die, such denial needs to change. At that point, those of my patients who have had the most peaceful, meaningful and dignified exits from mortal life started to ask something else. Those who were

able to enjoy their final moments and pass away in peace instead
asked, 'Since I cannot avoid dying, how I can I die well?'

As a society, the most exciting time in any family is
preparing for the birth of a child. For expecting parents, and to-
be grandparents, aunts and uncles, nothing matters more than
planning and getting ready for the arrival of a new member in
the family. Our lives change with baby showers, preparations
and an entirely different lifestyle to accommodate the needs
of the newborn. Yet, we don't show nearly the same degree of
preparation for our departure from this world. The fact that we
will depart someday is established the instant we are born. Still, an
unspoken taboo seems to forbid us from planning for a smooth,
graceful and celebratory death.

What is the meaning, value and concept of a good death?
When should we start thinking and talking about the process of
death and dying?

The moment a terminal illness like cancer is diagnosed, death
lurks beneath every discussion—at times addressed directly but
usually left unbroached. As physicians, it is our responsibility to
be the lighthouse that guides patients through the rough waters
that they are then forced to sail.

How do we prepare our patients for a good death? Is it possible
for us to rise above our own hopes, fears and vulnerabilities, and be
candid in preparing patients for death? How do we communicate
the truth about death? Can we define it in absolute terms, or is it
best communicated through metaphors or purposeful silence?

Is death as bad as what our fears make it out to be? Maybe.
Maybe not. Science has not been able to solve that mystery, and
it is highly doubtful it will ever be solved. The only people who
can answer that question are well past communicating with the
living. What we can do, though, is face our own reluctance and
hesitation to understand and accept our finitude and embrace
our mortality. We keep chasing the mirage of longevity instead of

gracefully preparing for our own inevitable exit from this world—
something that no one will ever escape.

We human beings know that we are going to die. The choices
we make are shaped in countless ways by how we think about
death, what we believe happens after death, and what death—
and life—ultimately means. So thinking about death is essential
to any reflection on human life, and it brings us face to face with
what it means in the face of finitude and loss. In what ways might
death threaten the meaning of our lives? And in what ways might
death make a meaningful life possible?

What does it mean to die well? Some people aspire to die as
consciously as possible, knowing that they are going to die and
wanting to experience each moment of it fully. This allows them
to say the things that need to be said, to get their affairs in order
and, perhaps, gain further insight into the nature of life and death.

The experience of dying is highly individualized. According to
author Ira Byock, 'Patients who died most peacefully and families
who felt enriched by the passing of a loved one tended to be
particularly active in terms of their relationships and discussions
of personal and spiritual matters.'*

Byock also found that 'good deaths' were not random events
or matters of luck. They could be fostered by the choices of the
dying person—choices that could achieve important goals, even
on death's doorstep. 'Even as they are dying,' Byock wrote, 'most
people can accomplish meaningful tasks and grow in ways that are
important to them and their families.'

There is great value in asking the question: 'Am I prepared to
die?' Let's consider what that preparation involves.

Most of us would admit that, in some way or the other, we
fear death. But what if we are making a mistake—an error of

---

* Ira Byock, *Dying Well: Peace and Possibilities at the End of Life* (New York:
Riverhead Books, 1998).

reason? What if our fear of death is based on a misconception that death, if corrected, would eliminate our fear? And what if that misconception were the belief that death is bad? Wouldn't we have lived an entire life fleeing a spectre that, in actuality, is terrible only through our own interpretation of it?

I have spent thousands of hours near death, with my patients. I have witnessed death in every shape and form. I have seen the young and the old, male and female, rich and poor, all die in different ways. Despite all the miracles of modern medicine, I've seen many people die even in the prime of their lives.

In this book, I share several of my own experiences with everyday people like you and me who were forced by cancer to face their own mortality. I have helped such patients prepare for the journey beyond life, along with aiding their families in coping with the loss and helping them all find closure in the time that God left to them. All of these patients had common anxieties and concerns:

How will I die?

What will happen to my body?

Will I be in pain?

Will I suffer?

Will I be in a coma?

Will I be able to feel touch? Will I be able to hear?

Will my body shiver?

Will I die a good death?

What shape will my body be once I die?

Will there be an afterlife? Is there a soul?

Will my family witness me passing and leaving this world?

It is my sincere hope and prayer that, without having to face the knowledge of a terminal illness, as these patients did before searching for their answers, you will find a comforting, and perhaps even peaceful, answer to your own questions as you read about how others faced theirs.

1

Destination Unknown

Hi, friends!

This email is different from my usual. No smiley faces or funny cartoons, for I have moved to another location.

I have often thought that life is rather like a queue at the departure level of a very huge airport. We all have our place in our individual queue, and from the moment we are born, we slowly but surely move towards the head of the line. There we take our turn to get checked out and receive a boarding pass to our next place.

My place in the long line of life has suddenly been jumped up to the head of the queue, and now I have a boarding pass. I want you to know that I am looking forward to adventures beyond this world. And I certainly don't want to join the many folks towards the head of the other queues, who are in beds, their frail bodies pierced with tubes, or limbs missing, or staring into nowhere with unseeing eyes—all of them waiting patiently for God.

I, on the other hand, have had an exciting and enjoyable life to the end. I have married three times (to my shame), and fathered six wonderful children. Now that I am approaching seventy-eight years of age, it's time to move on.

I just want to let my friends, whether close or far, dear friends or acquaintances, know that I have enjoyed passing on the smiles, which I know most of you have appreciated, and send to all of you my very best wishes for the future.

Live each day to the fullest.

Harry

As an oncologist, my profession had me witness death every day. I wrote this book to help patients and their families come to terms with what really takes place versus what they wished would happen.

As for any responsible physician, my patients were not mere names on a clipboard. This hit close to home when an associate brought me some news I was not prepared to hear.

My day started with a meeting with Stan Mueller, the Piedmont hospital CEO, and Susan McGill, the director of oncology services. After a brief discussion about community expansion of our office's oncology services, we closed, and I was about to leave when Susan quietly asked me for a minute of my time.

The slight hunch in her shoulders and the tremor in her voice told me something was wrong with my long-time friend and colleague.

She didn't say anything as we walked to the main hallway. Finally, we passed by the interfaith chapel, where Susan paused and reached into her briefcase. I wasn't prepared for the conversation that followed.

She handed me some papers, her hands shaking.

'Can you look this over and see what you think of this report?'

Somewhat relieved of the uncomfortable silence, I pushed my concerns about my friend to the back of my mind as the medical side of my brain took over. It was a chest X-ray and report for someone named Harry Falls.

> PA and lateral views of chest reveal a large right hilar mass with upper, middle and lower lobe infiltrates. The left lung appears normal. There is a mass effect on the hilum with right upper and lower lobe infiltrates. Suggest a follow-up enhanced chest CT.

In layman's terms, someone named Harry Falls had something very serious happening in his chest.

I started interpreting what the report indicated. The X-ray detected a spot overlying the middle of the right lung. There was also pneumonia involving the majority of the right lung tissues. It was bad news for Mr Falls.

I started the all-too-familiar spiel known to all oncologists. 'I would proceed with the CT scan and see what it shows, but my gut says that it doesn't look promising for Mr Falls. By the way, how do you know him?'

At that moment, her fear gave way to confusion and disappointment.

'What? Kashyap? Are you serious? This is Harry's X-ray! Harry! My husband Harry! Didn't you recognize him?'

I was taken aback. All I could muster was, 'I'm so sorry.'

I had known Susan and Harry for a long time. They were a devoted and loving couple. But I had never realized she had kept her maiden name after marriage . . . I had assumed that his name was Harry McGill.

I was already crestfallen that I hadn't been able to piece together that the scan belonged to my friend's husband. But worse, my initial response was cold and impersonal—a manifestation of the typical, detached, clinical manner that still periodically came up despite my conscious efforts to overcome it when talking to patients and families.

Susan placed her hand on my arm. 'It's okay. I should have explained who the reports belong to.'

Although her touch and understanding eased my guilt, it didn't erase it. Susan had been a colleague and a friend for more than five years. Perhaps I should have slowed down and thought before responding. Maybe I should have paused and asked more questions before speaking. Most alarmingly, it seemed that despite all my experience and training, sometimes I just wasn't prepared to handle such personal and delicate situations.

'What do you suggest we do next?' Susan asked.

'Let's carry out a CT of the lung and the liver, and probably a biopsy so that we can analyse the lesion in detail.'

'He has already scheduled a CT for Friday morning,' she replied. 'Will you take over his case?'

'Of course. Do you want to come to the office or should I join you for the X-ray before the procedure?'

'I need to talk to Harry. We'll meet you in the X-ray department.'

After we parted, my mind bounced between the hope that new oncology therapies were starting to offer and the harsh reality of what would likely happen. Cancer had just dropped a ticking time bomb on Susan and Harry's life together. Susan perhaps understood Harry's prognosis, even though I wasn't ready to verbally commit to anything. And now the personal questions began to traipse through my mind. Harry had been asking her to retire so they could enjoy their golden years doing what they loved, especially gliding, but she had postponed it. Would she come to regret that decision?

The usual course of the disease flashed through my mind. I had been unable to comfort Susan so far, and the journey had not even started. So many uncertainties lay ahead, along with questions that I had. It was premature to jump to any conclusion. We still had only the barest preliminary indication that this was most likely cancerous. What if it wasn't? My experience in treating cancer all these years had taught me one clear lesson: No one has a crystal ball to see into the future.

I squared my shoulders and tried to regain my composure. At this point, I could only pray to reign in my emotions so I could help my friends as they prepared to navigate the turbulence ahead.

On Friday morning, I reached the X-ray department early. Although I had prepared myself mentally and emotionally, my demeanour dissolved the moment I saw Harry breeze through the entrance, looking more amused than worried. Dressed in comfortable khakis and a crisp Oxford shirt, Harry eased into the department as if he were on holiday. But despite the air of carelessness he projected, the truth was evident in the changes I noticed in him. Wrinkles that weren't there the last time I had seen him forecasted what was coming. His body exhibited signs of muscle wasting, and his collarbone was visible through his crisp shirt. Something sinister was slowly eating away at his once-prominent muscle mass. And yet, in spite of Harry's cavalier attitude, I understood why Susan had fallen for him. Harry's smile illuminated his face and lifted the spirits of all around him.

He walked forward and extended his hand. 'Dr Patel!'

What was behind Harry's smile? How did he feel on the inside—the part that was sheltered from outside eyes? Was he in denial? I shook his outstretched hand. Harry appeared to be in control, even though his own physician wasn't. 'Hi, Harry. I'm here to help you in any way I can. If it's okay, I'd like to examine you as soon as you change into a gown.'

As he went to change, I found myself thinking about Harry and his life. He was an avid glider pilot. Harry's hobby suggested that he was someone with a particularly brave mentality. Still, Harry was notable even among that community, having earned three diamonds—one of the highest awards for glider instructors. To attain this distinction, Harry had demonstrated exceptional skill, and he was accustomed to adjusting to difficult situations. But now he was being forced to prepare for uncharted skies. What would happen when he was forced to navigate a hospital environment known for stripping people of all control and placing them in the hands of fate?

Once Harry had changed, I conducted a brief physical examination on him and questioned him about his health. Apart from weakness and episodes of dry cough, Harry said he had been feeling reasonably well. Further questions revealed he had experienced occasional discomfort on the right side of his chest and had lost almost twenty pounds.

To Harry, the symptoms appeared minor because they had only slightly slowed his active lifestyle. But with each answer, my concerns increased. His sunken eyeballs, the visible dimples on his facial bones and the clear sagging of his shoulders due to decreased muscle mass all revealed a hidden enemy inside him—one that was slowly but steadily consuming his body. Upon pressing his belly, I found that Harry's liver was quite enlarged, and he sighed in pain from the pressure I had applied on his right side just below the ribs. Although I was avoiding presumptive diagnosis until I could collect all of the test results and biopsies, Harry's chest X-rays, coupled with his symptoms and my physical examination, pointed to a grim prognosis and a difficult discussion to come.

As I completed the examination, I explained that I was sending him for a CT (computerized tomography) scan.

Harry stretched out on an automated table that would move back and forth into a small tunnel that contained the scanner. The technician inserted an intravenous catheter into his arm and connected the line to a rapid dispenser to inject a controlled amount of dye through Harry's body. Once the tech completed the initial set-up, he joined Susan and me in an adjacent room to await the live images the scanner would transmit of Harry's lungs and liver.

Harry was quickly moved in and out of the small tunnel that rotated around his body. Within minutes the screen in our viewing room displayed Harry's body. As each image flashed across the screen, I wondered if Susan, standing at my side, could read my anxiety and my internal struggle as I interpreted what I was seeing.

I had worked very hard over the years to refrain from attaching emotions to patients. I had never been fully successful. Over time, I had learned that increasing my effort to remain emotionally detached only increased my sense of abject failure at it. Today was worse. Today I didn't have time to compose myself or frame the results with compassion. This dear friend of mine needed all of my skill and empathy, since the situation turned out much worse than I had previously imagined.

'Wait a minute. Back up,' I ordered the technician.

'It's just artefact.'

'Nope. Back it up.'

The images on the screen reversed. I pointed at the screen. 'There. Can you magnify and highlight that spot?'

'Yeah, I see it. Okay, there it is.' A tiny bright spot enlarged and then came into focus on the screen.

Susan moved closer. 'What organ is it?' The two-syllable word hung in my throat almost as if I were choking before I managed to respond. 'Liver.'

'Stage?'

I was torn between being honest with her and wanting to give her hope. I couldn't dash all of her hopes in this dark room. Besides, staging was too important for error. What if I was wrong?

And yet, I knew I wasn't. I swallowed hard.

'Likely stage 4.'

'Stage 4' meant that the cancer was inoperable and had already spread to multiple tissues. In the resulting deathly silence in the room, the visual images continued to flicker on the screen. Sickened at what was displayed on the screen, I completed my mental interpretation of the results.

A large tumour had invaded Harry's right lung, and multiple small tumours covered the liver. Although I had dictated similar reports often in the past, this was different. Those same few words that I had read and dictated and explained to patients hundreds of times now meant my friend's life and death. Those few report lines would dictate how much time he had left on earth. Worse, the bad news didn't stop there.

The appearance of the tumour, the type of pressure effects it had created, and its rapid spread to the liver suggested the likelihood of small-cell cancer. Small-cell cancer is particularly virulent. It spreads like wildfire and engulfs all tissues in its path.

Breaking the silence that had pervaded the room since I had mentioned the words 'stage 4', I said, 'I think the best course is a biopsy, so we know what we're dealing with exactly.' This was the right approach: Focus on the appropriate clinical treatment path.

Susan didn't reply. Her chin just dropped towards her chest.

The dimmed lighting of the imaging room enhanced her pallor. As a member of the hospital treatment board, she'd seen and heard discussion of similar images in the past. We both had been through this journey with many patients. However, seeing it and living it were two dreadfully different tasks.

I put my hand on her shoulder. 'I'll make arrangements for the biopsy.'

Susan nodded.

For now, I had to focus on the facts, on the brick and mortar of the case. Until I had a tissue specimen, everything was still an assumption. Many thoughts raced through my mind as I scheduled Harry's appointment for a liver biopsy the next morning.

Harry's case and its implications occupied my mind for the rest of the evening. How many similar cases had I assessed prognosis and treatment options for? A hundred? Two hundred? How many of those cases had left me feeling as if I had just fallen from one of Harry's gliders?

Although I had always believed I was a compassionate oncologist, I now understood that I had to distinguish between being a friend and being an oncologist. I had to maintain distance and yet offer enough proximity to encourage my friends as well as myself. Cancer had touched not only my friends, but also me—in a new and profound way. Worse, I knew the path in front of Susan and Harry. That knowledge further dampened my spirits.

The next morning, I parked in the vast asphalt lot adjacent to my clinic. I didn't turn off the ignition or open the car's door. I knew what was waiting for me at the office. I had to make sure I was composed before I could lead my friends down this new path that fate had forced upon them.

My clinic, Carolina Blood and Cancer Care Associates, was founded on a holistic approach to the treatment of cancer. We had constructed the building in a U-shaped design that would allow all patients to look out to a healing garden with a gazebo with a golden dome. When the weather permitted, patients could receive their chemotherapy treatments outside on the patio or under the dome.

It wasn't just for the patients' comfort. During difficult discussions, a quick glance at the garden in bloom or the smile of a patient resting in the sun grounded me, put life in perspective, and reminded me of my mission of service.

After five minutes of quiet solitude in my sedan, I finally summoned the composure to walk into our waiting room. Harry and Susan were there. He was entirely composed, watching the fish in our small aquarium. I couldn't tell if he was just blissfully unaware of what was coming or whether he was in complete control. I welcomed them and walked Harry towards my consulting office, where I offered him a seat in a maroon guest chair across from my desk. I paused briefly and stole a glance at the garden. Peeking from above the slant of the roof, the morning sun illuminated a cloudless azure sky. And yet, the leafless plants and bare branches of winter added a solemn note to the wonderful weather.

Harry sat calmly. As I observed him, he continued to break my expectations of patient behaviour. Less than twenty-four hours ago, I had explained that he had a lung tumour and suspicious spots on his liver. Usually, even patients with no connection or knowledge of clinical terms recognized the gravity of the situation. And here he was—sitting blissfully. Was my friend in denial? Maybe I hadn't made myself clear.

I finally took a seat.

Harry's gaze was steady and his eyes met mine as he asked, 'What do you think it is?'

'I'm afraid it's likely cancer. And my instinct says it's a very aggressive form. As soon as we find out the type of cancer it is, we'll start you on chemotherapy and try to get you into remission.'

'What if I don't take chemo? How long do you think I can push on without doing anything?'

For a moment, I froze. This was an extremely peculiar discussion. Even when I saw patients in highly advanced cases, where I knew they were better off dying peacefully than going through the pain of chemotherapy—which bought them maybe a few more weeks—almost everyone was adamant in hoping for a miracle.

But Harry was different.

I didn't want to offer advice before I knew what exactly Harry had. I tried to bring some calm to my voice before answering, 'I'm not God, and I don't have a crystal ball. Even if I did, right now it's covered with dust. Let's wait until we have the biopsy results so I can have a more informed conversation.'

'If you say so, doc. From what I've heard from Susan, I trust you.'

I appreciated Harry's confidence, but as the conversation continued, covering treatment options and anticipated outcomes, a heaviness weighed on my spirit. I care deeply about every patient, and years of experience do not make these conversations any easier. Harry's naturally calm and emotionless demeanour contrasted with what I actually felt, as I fought to retain my own. I was almost relieved when he stood up to leave.

Was Harry in denial? Apathetic? My limited social interactions with him weren't of any help in understanding his reaction. To effectively treat the mental aspects of the disease, I needed to understand Harry's psychology. Was he just going through the stage of disbelief?

Now alone in my office, I thought back to everything I had heard from Susan about her husband's life. Born in England, Harry had fought in two wars and travelled around the world. He was Susan's gliding instructor, and had taken her on her first flight. She had always talked about his competence and ability to maintain control of the situation even when gliding thousands of feet in the air. Was this what I'd witnessed today?

Two hours after the Monday-morning biopsy, Harry and Susan were in my office again. Susan's outward composure had returned since our first encounter, but she couldn't conceal the shadows beneath her eyes that spoke of a sleepless weekend. Harry, true to form, appeared as normal as ever.

He looked straight into my eyes and asked, 'What's the verdict? Am I heading for a soft landing? Sorry . . . I'm a pilot. I like flight metaphors.'

I squared my shoulders and replied, 'I'm sorry, Harry. You have extensive-stage small-cell lung cancer.'

Susan's face went pale. Harry took a few short breaths, then let out a soft sigh. 'What next?' he said.

'There are some excellent and effective treatment options available. With these treatments, there's a real possibility of adding quality and extending your life.'

I wanted to reassure him, but I also wanted to buy a few minutes before the next question came, which, from experience, I knew would be about life expectancy.

'How long do I have if I do nothing and just let nature take its course?'

I paused. I guess he hadn't been in denial when he had asked me the same thing on Friday. The question was difficult to answer. In my field, blunt honesty was always more difficult than hiding behind a complex scientific response. 'Median survival is six months. Some patients die in weeks, while some live up to a year. There's no way to predict what's coming our way. Why don't we consider our treatment options?'

After a brief silence, Harry asked, 'What are my options?'

As I explained every possible course of treatment we could take for Harry's illness, including complications he may face, likely responses and, finally, possible outcomes, my glance jumped between Harry and Susan. She knew this conversation—after all, she had taken an active role in similar conversations in the past with patients at the hospital. But somehow, I doubted that those previous conversations had prepared her for today. I doubted if she was registering anything. Her eyes became moist, her breathing heavier.

We covered everything they needed to know. Harry finally stood up and extended his hand. 'Thanks for your patience, doc. I need some time to digest this. My entire life seems to have flashed by these last few minutes. I'll get back to you later in the week.'

The next day I found Harry and Susan in our waiting room. The corners of Susan's mouth was arched downwards, and her eyes were swollen and bloodshot. Even worse, I could see the resignation in the sag of her shoulders and her ashen complexion. My heart hurt for my friend. She appeared too vulnerable and frail to discuss treatment options and life expectancy for Harry.

Harry was standing, but Susan avoided eye contact and remained seated as I approached.

Harry then broke the silence. 'I'd like to discuss something with you in private. Would you mind talking to me without Susan present?'

The request was quite unusual, especially given how close I knew the couple to be. However, since Susan's gaze remained on the carpet, I had no choice but to respect Harry's request. As I led the way to my office, I couldn't help wondering, 'Why exclude Susan?' Susan and Harry were partners, and both had a role to play in the difficult journey ahead.

Inside my office, I gestured towards the guest chair and turned to my seat behind the desk. Outside, the sun topped the trees and filtered on to the concrete patio. Harry seemed to notice the weather and paused to admire the cloudless sky. Did he understand that his time of gliding in the skies was drawing to a close?

He exhaled and settled into the chair. 'After evaluating where I stand and how I've lived all these years, I feel it would be best for me to start packing my bags for the ultimate and infinite journey.'

He pointed towards the window.

'I've been on many flights high up in the sky, quite close to my eventual destination. I have flown and chased hawks, and have even dared to be among the soaring eagles. God blessed me with a life that I have no regrets over, and I don't want my life ending in any other way than that.'

I was floored. 'I agree with your philosophy, but God also gave us treatments for disease. Maybe . . . '

'Yes, but I think God wants me to look at this milestone of cancer and realize it's time to seek and explore a different world. I don't want to defy or interfere with His plan for me. I welcome my destination. It's time for me to check in for my final flight, and I'll gladly await His boarding call. That's why I don't want treatment.'

I moistened my lips. 'But treatment could buy more time.'

'Treatment with known side effects.'

'We have good drugs to help minimize the side effects.'

'Minimize.'

'Different people respond differently. There's no guarantee, but . . . '

'Let's face it, doc. From everything you've told me, treating my cancer is like trying to save an exploding plane in mid-air. Chances are it's not going to happen.'

Although I felt like the world had tipped a little, Harry was in perfect control of his emotions. Like a solo pilot experiencing minor turbulence on a plane, he had recovered his composure from our previous meeting.

His voice didn't waver, and his steady gaze never left my eyes except to periodically glance outside at his world—the cloudless sky.

'I need to prepare Susan and my lovely daughters for this. I've always enjoyed flying high. And I've been in control all my life. I'd like to go out that way too.'

'That's understandable,' I said.

He went on, explaining his thoughts. 'I think of it like I've just received an upgrade on a long flight. I've collected so many miles that God has granted me a charter flight to a destination unknown. Now the only issue is the waiting time.'

I hesitated, unsure where Harry was going with the conversation.

'I need to know one thing,' he said.

'Yes?'

'Will you help me in making this transition into my new life easier for my family, so memories of my last days aren't painful for them but something they can cherish?'

I released the breath I hadn't realized I was holding. Harry's request was one I could grant. 'Of course. We can consult home hospice. They can give you and Susan the logistical support you'll need.'

'Not just that. I knew you would be able to help me with hospice. I need more than that.' Harry sounded like he was in complete control. He was the one guiding this conversation. Fitting, considering he had always been the pilot.

'I'll do my best not to disappoint you with whatever I can help you with.'

'Help me. I've never seen death before. Tell me what you know about it, what you've seen. What was it like to witness your patients leaving this world? Tell me how you coped with it. Aren't you afraid of death yourself?'

He paused.

I'm sure my eyebrows rose as I tried to understand his questions. My mind started speeding, trying to decipher his questions and form vague explanations.

Before I could say anything, he continued, 'I do not intend to question your experience or judgement. I want to learn from your experiences. How have you been able to elevate yourself above the misery of the permanent separation from so many patients you care about so dearly, the many folks like me whom you've had to say goodbye to? You enter your patients' lives, become part of their world. We hand over our lives to you and give you permission to inject poisonous chemicals into us that can even potentially kill us before cancer does. How do you find the courage to prepare the people you care about for a permanent separation and departure? How do you manage to deal with this? Does dealing with death not affect you, your personal life?'

'Sorry, let me rephrase that,' Harry went on. 'Have you seen your patients on their deathbeds, actually bidding them goodbye when they left their mortal remains behind? I doubt many doctors in the US make home visits. Susan told me that you are one of those rare doctors who do so on a regular basis. All I want to see is whether I can prepare for my own death. Can I prepare my dear wife and daughters? Two of my children are still in the land down under, back in Australia.'

Now I knew where he was heading. 'Yes, Harry, I've seen many departures from this world, and that, too, in many ways— from being chained to an IV on an ICU hospital bed, groaning in extreme pain, to gracefully giving way in the comfort of holding their loved ones' hands. I've seen young and old, rich and poor, beautiful and plain, white, black, Asian and Indian. I have seen all the dimensions of death. I have learnt the anatomy and physiology of death. I have mulled over the philosophy of death.

'Even before I pursued oncology, I smelt the ashes of people burnt alive in riots when I was an ER physician in India. I've seen the torture of dying from stab wounds as a result of gang wars during my residency in Jamaica, Queens.'

Harry was visibly distressed at the violent deaths I had experienced. I changed my tone.

'However, I have also smelt the sweet aroma of sandalwood on funeral pyres, surrounded by loving family as their relatives were cremated, and the family had a chance to say goodbye. I have witnessed many funeral ceremonies. I even lit the funeral pyre of my own brother.

'I have seen death in every possible shape, form, colour and dimension. I have narrowly escaped death from a heart attack myself. I grew up in the shadow of my father, a man who, even though he was not a doctor, was forced to witness almost everyone near and dear die from as young as four years of age, so much so that when my brother died at the age of forty-three, he had no tears left—he had shed them all sending off his loved ones. He had eulogized so many of his loved ones that when his own son passed, he didn't even have words left to express his grief.'

The corners of my eyes got wet and my voice trembled a little.

'I'm so sorry,' Harry said. He had perhaps not anticipated that his question would bring up some of my worst memories. 'I never wanted to remind you of old sorrows. I'm sorry,' he said as his voice wavered.

'Please don't apologize, Harry. As an oncologist, it's always been my job to guide patients through their grief. I can't burden people facing death themselves with my sorrows at death's hands. I try not to burden my own family and try to even shelter my dear wife from it. Sometimes, I wake up in the middle of the night, questioning my own judgement about what I have learnt. I should thank you . . . I rarely have an outlet for my own grief. I appreciate your candour, trust and faith. I promise I will not disappoint you in sharing what I have learnt through my life as best I can.'

I put my own grief aside as I smiled at him.

'I've seen the funeral sites of prehistoric Neolithic settlements of the Indus Valley civilization in Lothal, in my home state in India,' I said. 'I've seen the ancient pyramids of Giza in Egypt, the final resting place of the pharaohs. I've visited the holy city of Jerusalem. I've studied the Mayan culture. What all these ancient sites show us is that humankind, even thousands of years ago, tried to make sense of and come to terms with death—long before the two of us here in Rock Hill, South Carolina, are trying to come to terms with it. I'll do my best to help you.'

'Thanks, doc. I need to know what happens when people die. I'd like to know so that I can plan my exit. I want to go in celebration, not gloom.' Harry seemed to grow more comfortable around the subject as he spoke about his questions.

He continued, 'My wife always told me that you were great with counselling your patients near their end, and that you interspersed spirituality and philosophy with science. Having been raised in a different culture, your religious beliefs are different from mine, but I'd like to hear those too. I'm not sure I will understand everything you say or explain. I'm not even sure I'll have the heart to hear all of it. But whatever knowledge, understanding, experiences and beliefs you share, in whichever format you do, will help me.'

'Yes, I can definitely share my journey with you. I will also share some of my other patients' stories with you, if you believe they will help. Maybe we can both learn something from the stories I have witnessed.'

I paused.

'When do you want to begin?'

'Maybe we can meet once a week around lunchtime, here, under this beautiful copper dome. Could we start tomorrow?' Harry sounded more than a little relieved.

'Sure. Where do you want me to begin? Real-life stories? Young? Old? ICU? Hospice? Or home?'

'First, tell me about your father. It's obvious that he's had a great influence on you. Tell me how he helped you become fearless.'

2

The Cycle of Life and Death

The body is made of worldly stuff
It comes, lingers and goes
The Self neither comes nor goes
It remains forever; why thee grieve then?
You are not the body, nor do you have a body
You are awareness only; True awareness
You are eternal, blissful awareness.

—Ashtavakra

The next day, by lunchtime, with Harry in my office, I pointed to a photograph on my office shelf. It featured an old Indian man in his early eighties; his face was dark and covered with scars, but they didn't hide the smile that was still glowing with hope.

It was the face of a man who had witnessed many deaths—the face of one who had lived with death since the age of four. The scars were from a childhood spent working the fields while his friends played.

'That is my father,' I said. 'I spent my formative years under his guidance and wisdom. He was forced to cremate his father when he was four, his mother when he was ten and his younger brother when he was in his thirties. When it was time for him to deliver his son's eulogy, he couldn't even cry, having lost all his tears to grief long ago. And yet, no matter the extent of his grief, he never gave up his trust, faith or optimism. He is the source of my strength and resilience. He is the one who instilled fearlessness in me.'

I fought a lump in my throat as I recalled my father's struggle.

'He looks a lot different now. Even he is now slowly awaiting his infinite and ultimate journey. After sending off his own loved ones, he's getting ready for his own departure.'

'Is he ill?' Harry asked.

'No, he isn't physically ill. But he has given up now. He feels that his role in this world is over. He wants to pull the curtains on the final act of his passing. His lungs have been damaged from years of exposure to asbestos, and his work building roads in dusty, remote areas of India left him with chronic obstructive pulmonary disease (COPD). He has lost his strength and can barely walk ten feet a day, but he still has not lost his smile. Like an old tree, he is ridding himself of all possessions. And slowly, he's giving up on his activities and his interests.'

'A tragic but interesting life,' Harry mused. But I could tell he did not want to hear about individual suffering. Perhaps he didn't want to envision himself approaching a similar fate in the near future.

Then Harry came to the same point with which we had concluded the previous day's visit.

'Tell me how your dad helped you become fearless.'

We took our seats. As I took a deep breath, I probed my memory back to the day we had driven through the jungle.

Almost thirty years ago, I was travelling to a remote tribal village in India with my father, who was then one of the foremost construction engineers working for the state government. He built roads and bridges. We were in a rugged twenty-year-old Jeep on a hot Indian summer day. I was sitting in the front beside the car's driver. We heard a strange whizzing sound from the engine. The radiator had started leaking from a small, rusted hole. The driver pulled out a bar of cheap soap and smeared it on the hole, hoping that it would last until we reached a repair shop. The whizzing continued, although it was less intense, and the driver periodically reapplied the soap.

A few miles ahead, we came across some leaves on the road. As the car passed over the leaves, it began swerving from side to side. It turned out that one of the leaves had had a large nail underneath it, and it had punctured the rear tyre. Nomadic people living in that area used to hide nails on the road to cause tyre bursts so they could loot the stranded travellers. There we were, on a lonely jungle road, in a car with a burst tyre and a radiator held together with soapsuds.

The driver nervously got out of the car to change the tyre, looking over his shoulder the entire time. Once he was done with the repairs, we continued towards a thick jungle that was known for wild bears. With the others busy discussing and looking for tell-tale signs of bears, I grew nervous and worried.

My father noticed my anxiety and asked, 'Son, what is bothering you?' Embarrassed, I told him it was nothing. But he knew that something was wrong.

He asked again, 'You look worried. Are you scared?'

I acquiesced and admitted, 'Yes, Dad, I'm scared. We're so far away from civilization in this jungle, and no one knows if bandits will come and rob us or if a bear will come and attack us. We have nothing to protect us at all.'

My father responded reassuringly, 'Son, we are never far from help. The earth has given us its fruits and sustained us like a loving mother. No matter where we are, we are always in the lap of Mother Earth. Why should we ever be scared in the lap of our mother? You are at home in every part of this world, no matter how strange or scary some parts may seem; it is all part of the nourishing whole that has supplied us with life. The Almighty always watches over His creations and will look after us in whatever corner of the world we may be in.'

This wasn't very convincing to my scared young mind. 'That's all well and good, but I see no one nearby,' I said. 'I don't see how we are safe here like we are at home.'

'No, son, what I am saying is true and is supported by geometry. You need to apply the broader context of knowledge. It is all about perspective.'

This made no sense to me. 'What do you mean?'

'Is Earth a sphere?' he asked me.

'Yes,' I replied.

'So, any point on it can be considered the centre of its surface perimeter?'

'Yes. But I don't see how geometry, in any way, offers protection from robbers or bears.'

'I am not done explaining yet. What is the most important thing a mother does for her child after giving birth?'

'Feeds it her own milk. Nurtures him or her.'

'And where do you get your food from?'

'From the fruit and vegetable market!' I answered.

'No, that is where you buy it from. Where did those fruits and vegetables grow?'

'Soil?'

'Yes. Now then, isn't soil part of the perimeter of this earth? Is it not true that the soil of the earth feeds you for your entire life— even longer than your own mother? Is this not nature's maternal instinct?'

'You can say so.'

'Isn't it true, then, that right now you are in the centre of the lap of your mother? Someone who has fed you selflessly for much longer than your own biological mother?'

'Yes, it is true,' I conceded. But this only led to another question. 'But why would she care about me? She has to feed everyone on this planet.'

'Why should that matter? No loving mother would leave any of her children hungry, even if she had two, five or ten. All her children hold an equal place in her heart. Similarly, Mother Earth sustains life for all living beings. So she will protect and look after you wherever and whenever she can. In every place in the world, people are made of and fed by the same soil of Mother Earth. You should never feel unsafe anywhere on this planet.'

I paused and looked at Harry. He looked puzzled—maybe he got what my father meant, maybe not.

I said, 'At the time, his message didn't come through and I was still scared. Eventually, we made it out fine, and no man or animal attacked us. But later, in many instances in life, I have thought back to those words whenever I have been frightened or upset. And even to this day, whenever something scares me, I remember his words. Maybe that is why I don't get terrified any more.'

Harry said, 'I'd like to meet him someday. He sounds truly inspiring.'

'He is almost ten thousand miles away. And I don't think we'll have the luxury of travelling to India.' I wanted to be sure that the discussion didn't blind Harry to the finite time we were up against.

'Well, doc, even if we can't go to India, I think these talks are going to do me some good,' Harry said.

'I should warn you, Harry, I love to talk—and if I have an audience, I am unstoppable!' I said.

He smiled mischievously. 'Nowadays, they prepare your body to make you look almost alive. If my mortal remains are prepared as if I am ready for a party, why not prepare my brain as well?'

Conversation lapsed for several moments as we both gazed out at the peaceful garden landscape. I couldn't help thinking, 'Harry, you're a risk-taker, a pilot and a gliding instructor for people who love soaring to new heights. So why don't you want to explore treatment options? If anyone has the stomach for a fight, it is you.'

Cancer strips away the guise of immortality and makes its victims face the fact that death is an inevitable, integral part of life. With a terminal illness, one has a good prediction of how and when. This knowledge allows the time to prepare for one's passing and to appreciate one's life and loved ones. Treatment can offer more of that precious time to get one's affairs in order and spend what time remains around those one loves.

Unlike in a sudden mid-air crash, Harry had the opportunity to savour time as the hawk soaring on the current, to appreciate the gentleness of Susan's touch, and to tell his daughters, Patricia and Holly, the depth of his feelings before he passed away. He had the time to make amends for past regrets and prevent new ones.

Outside, a small cloud covered the sun. I took a deep, cleansing breath. Maybe Harry was right. God gave people free will so they could make their own choices. Harry had made his and I would respect it. I would also honour Harry's request to facilitate the end stages of his disease for Susan and his daughters.

For our next visit, Harry arrived on time, dressed with his usual care in a pristine, neatly pressed collared shirt. His steps through the hallway echoed his usual confidence, and he shook my hand with a firmness that, having seen his reports, took me by surprise.

'Ready to get started, doc?'

'Sure, Harry. Let's step outside and sit under the healing dome.'

We exited the building and sat among the brightly blooming flowers and the trickling fountain.

'So, Harry, how was your day? Has anything changed since we last met?'

'Yes and no,' Harry said.

I couldn't tell yet whether he was depressed or jovial. But his next words left little doubt.

'A lot has changed since we met last week,' he continued. 'I have started visualizing my corpse and how I want to look inside my hearse. I can't fathom how, since time immemorial, no one has managed to conquer death! I just can't come to terms with this simple fact.'

Harry was frustrated. 'We have the capacity to send rockets to Mars, and yet have no clue about predicting our time of death. Can we delay or avoid it? Like cryotherapy suggests, can we freeze the body for a period of time and then bring it back to life? I'm disappointed in medicine and science. Do I sound crazy to ask all these questions?'

I took a deep breath and tried to give him a reassuring smile.

'Harry, not at all,' I said. 'Your reaction is quite normal, and this is what I see every day in my patients. These questions have haunted intelligent life on this planet ever since we can trace it back to our ancestors. But before I share what I have learnt about your questions, let me tell you something about the role cancer plays in life.'

John Lennon wrote, 'Life is what happens to you while you're busy making other plans.' Nothing could be truer when someone is told they have cancer. All plans come to a screeching halt when something puts a tangible deadline on life. A person with cancer—and those who love and support him or her—is cast into a world that grows increasingly complicated, frightening and daunting. It can crush the human spirit.

And yet, it's that very human spirit that is needed more than ever to offer the greatest chance to healing. That's how we see it. It's why an integral part of the science of treating cancer has always been discovering better ways to help people live with the disease. It's a focus that causes us, as physicians, to keep the individuals affected by cancer, and those who care for them, at the centre of our efforts—so that, on those days when life happens, they can cope with it.

Every type of cancer affects the heart. Not the heart that pumps blood through our body, but the heart that helps us live a life filled with hope and fulfilment. The heart that gives us a vital link to those we love and those who love us. And when cancer spreads to that heart, the damage can be just as devastating as anything that begins in our cells.

I try never to forget that. In fact, it is the reason we keep those who live with cancer and those who care for them at the centre of everything we do. It is why, in addition to our relentless search for scientific breakthroughs, we strive to discover new ways of caring. It is how we show that we are dedicated to every human heart that is touched by cancer.

Consider the moment of a cancer diagnosis. It's a lonely moment of distress, and its unfairness can be heard as patients think, 'Why me?'

But when you think about it, death has surrounded all living beings since the beginning of time. We forget that the beautiful autumn leaves that fall from trees are at the close of their life span. We admire the sight of fireflies, forgetting that most of them live for just a few precious hours before being consumed by birds. But we forget to see death in that.

We breathe in and breathe out life and death every day. Life and death are so closely woven together that they are two sides of the same coin. The air we breathe was once part of a life form, and the elements of carbon, oxygen and nitrogen that formulated its body were recycled back in the environment after the organism died. The iron in our blood, the calcium in our bones and the water we drink may even have been part of the mortal remains of a star that died millions or billions of years ago.

Every second, every minute and every hour in a cycle that may last forever, life keeps recycling in the face of death.

Harry interjected, 'This may be a good explanation for those who live on a different level of awareness. But what about ordinary people like me? I have witnessed a drastic change in my attitude towards death. I don't recall anxiety about death in my own parents and grandparents. I'm not sure what changed since I grew up, that I now have all these questions about death. My grandmother died at home almost seventy years back and I saw my parents preparing her body for the funeral. I don't recall anyone dying at home these days. Everyone dies in hospital and then they go straight to the funeral home.

'I don't have any memories of how people died and what happened to their bodies. I was too young to remember then and never witnessed it after. What about you? Has your practice of treating people after they die changed as well? I know I ask too many questions. I'm anxious to know about this so I can prepare myself for a good death, and also control how my body is prepared after death and how I prepare my family for life after my passing.'

I reassured Harry, 'My friend, you don't need to justify your questions. I get it.'

He continued, 'When I was a pilot with the Royal Air Force, I always planned ahead and tried to remain in control. I know these questions and comments sound repetitive. I want to plan my own funeral. But I feel helpless here—this is uncharted territory. I want to rehearse my own process of dying and the release of my soul. I want to visualize what will happen once I stop breathing.

How will my dear wife Susan react? I want to minimize the pain and suffering of both myself and my family.'

'And I'm here to help you do just that, Harry,' I said. 'I will do my very best to prepare you and minimize the painful part of the process.'

Harry went on. 'Doc, I'm not a religious or ritualistic individual. I'm somewhere between a non-believer and an agnostic. But I have some fundamental existential queries that are haunting me. I am not sure if I will live long enough to get answers to all of them. At the very least, I want to know how death has been defined all these millennia. How do people die? Did our ancestors understand death like we do? How did they treat the bodies after death? How was this different across cultures? What about the afterlife? What is a good death—or rather, what does it mean to die well?

'I can handle a mid-air somersault and navigate the worst turbulence, but I am incapable of even remotely imagining my own mortality and afterlife. Do I sound crazy?'

'Not at all, Harry!' I assured him again. 'I wish everyone facing death—which is, in fact, everyone someday—would spend time thinking about these questions. For some reason, modern medicine has lulled us into feeling that death is an option and that it only happens on television or in some third-world country. We are relatively free of starvation, cholera, malaria, terrorism or civil wars that force us to see death every day. But still, we all live with the certainty that we will die one day. The only uncertainty is when. And since we do not know when, we live in the illusion of immortality. We have lost the sight, feel, touch, sense and smell of death in our vicinity.'

Suddenly, we were both startled by the sight of a long, black snake slithering through the grass a few feet outside the domed gazebo.

'Do you think it's poisonous?' Harry asked, keeping his eyes on our reptilian visitor.

'I don't know. Based on what I know about snakes from books, I'd guess it's non-poisonous.'

Harry may have been brave in the skies, but it was obvious that he did not like snakes. He shifted to an alert position in his chair and kept watching closely as the snake continued its journey across the garden.

I decided to turn this into a teachable moment.

'Actually, these black snakes eat other reptiles as well as bothersome rodents. They even attack small copperheads that are, in fact, dangerous. In a way, they are our guardians. I know there is a small snake pit in the woods behind our dome. We leave them alone, and they leave us alone.'

'I would have killed them if I were you.'

Harry wasn't getting my point yet.

'You see, Harry, snakes and the other creatures that live in this yard have been here for several millennia. They were here long before I bought the deed to the property, and they have the first right to living here. In fact, we are the intruders. I appreciate them allowing us to be here. They do not harm us, and we live in biological symbiosis. As long as they do not harm us, we do not disrupt their life either. I am not sure if snakes, roaches, butterflies or bats understand us. They may look at us like we are cancer, since we take over their territory—we metastasize and establish our habitats where they used to live before. Perhaps regard us as an aberrational life form that has gone berserk and is taking over their planet!'

'Okay,' Harry said, relaxing again now that our visitor had moved along. 'I think I get the metaphor.'

I chuckled and said, 'Sorry for the digression. Where were we?'

'No problem, doc,' Harry said. 'Let me summarize what I need to accomplish over the few weeks that I have left in this physical body. I want to first plan my death; I want to die at home, quietly, peacefully and gracefully. However, I do not want my wife or daughter to see my final moments. I do not want to be in pain. I do not want to suffer. I don't mind a morphine drip if necessary.'

I nodded, making mental notes.

'I want to learn about post-death rituals,' Harry said. 'How will they treat my body? Not for myself, but I want to help make the right choices so that my beloved family knows what exactly to do with my mortal remains. I want to learn about cremation versus burial, so I can choose the right method for myself. I want to minimize the mourning of my loved ones.

'And now, I am moving out of both of our comfort zones. If you have any experience of a connection to the afterlife with any of your patients, I want to hear about it. If you have not, but still believe in it, I want to know about it. Do you believe in the existence of the soul? Do you believe in reincarnation?'

Harry finally stopped. He had presented quite a list. I knew he would have further questions as we continued our conversations, but, for now, I felt the need to pause, summarize and assure him that perhaps my experiences watching terminal patients face death would help him find peace amid all the unknowns.

'Harry,' I said, 'your questions are quite natural for someone like you, who has been in the habit of planning all his life. I will do my best to share my experience, knowledge and reflections to help you discover the art of dying well. I will share real-life stories of my patients, which I think you will find very helpful. The only thing I cannot give you is the assurance of when you will die or how. This is outside anyone's control. And we will try to conduct these conversations in a well-planned manner, to maximize your learning and help you plan and prepare for each phase of passage from this world. Along the way, I will share my own beliefs. They are my personal convictions, but that's all they are. You don't need to embrace them unless, of course, you feel you should. But it may help you to hear them.'

'I'm in,' Harry said. 'Thank you again, doc. Next Wednesday?'

'Next Wednesday, same time,' I agreed.

'And, doc?' Harry said, pushing himself out of his chair. 'Can you clear out the snakes by then?'

3

What Is Death?

Death is certain for those who are born
For the deceased, rebirth is certain.
Since neither can be avoided, grieve not you!
Before birth, all beings are unmanifest
Between birth and death, they manifest again.
Upon death, beings unmanifest again
Why do you grieve then, for death?

—*Bhagavad Gita*

The following Wednesday, Harry showed up at noon, and we strolled together to the healing garden and dome. The sky was somewhat overcast. Although spring was around the corner, leafless branches of crepe myrtles with fresh seeds were rubbing against the copper dome, breaking the silence with occasional screeches. The tall magnolia on the other side of the dome contrasted the mood, with its lush green leaves, showing that life thrived even in the stark winter.

'Doc,' Harry began, taking control of the conversation like a captain, 'I've thought a lot about what we've discussed, and I have been able to crystallize my thoughts and inquisitiveness. What do your patients think and feel about death? What do they want to be done to their bodies after they die? I don't just want to hear about the biology, but the physiology, psychology, philosophy and evolution of our understanding on all these aspects of death.'

'Sure, my friend. While I do not claim to be an authority, I have learnt and studied about death in multiple dimensions so I can help those who seek my counsel. You see, Harry, we cannot confine our understanding about death to one simple scientific narrative or definition. Even when we look at a very narrow and reductionist approach to defining biological death, it is still a very broad narrative. That is why the definition of death has changed several times in the past few decades.'

'Interesting and also amusing, doc, that the definition of death has changed!'

'Indeed, it has. For example, for thousands of years, humanity believed that death occurred when a living being stopped breathing.'

'Wait—that's what I've always thought! So, what has changed?'

'You see, Harry, that has been the case throughout human history, going back to ancient Greece, Rome and even India. All these civilizations linked breath to life, to the point that they had a common word for "breath" and "life". Whether you take "pneumo" in ancient Greek, "ruach" in Hebrew, "spiritus" in Latin or "pran" in Sanskrit, they all implied life and breath as one. With the cessation of breath, life too came to an end, and the soul departed the body. This was the common understanding of life and death—that when we are born, our first inhalation brings life and our last exhalation brings death.'

I paused for a few moments to let that sink in and to formulate my next thoughts.

'The idea of linking life to breath helped humanity create a dualistic concept of existence and life. Over millennia, there have been many references, in archives as well as in remnants of past civilizations, to a strong belief in some form of afterlife. In a way, we can describe human beings in two parts—one that manifests into what we call a physical body upon birth, and the other that is a soul, which animates the physical body. Upon death, the soul leaves the body.'

Harry intervened, 'Well, for all these years, I've believed that death occurs when a person stops breathing. But I never felt certain about an afterlife. When did everything start changing?'

In the middle of the 1900s, as medicine advanced, the definition of death changed to cardiopulmonary death—which meant no heartbeat, no pulse and no respiration. As heart–lung machines and artificial respirators were developed, death came to mean no whole brain activity.

Further refinement to the definition of death came in 1985, when it was identified as the cessation of all activity in the brain, lungs and the heart. These refinements were the result of legal battles as well as a rise in cadaver organ donations and transplants.

Scientists have now started venturing into a new idea about death, and that is to link it to the most advanced part of the brain—the frontal brain, or the neocortex. Some neuroscientists believe that death occurs when the neocortex—or the centre of the brain, responsible for awareness in a human being—stops functioning. So even when the heart is functioning, even when the person is breathing, even when his small brain or brain stem is functioning, with the loss of function of the neocortex, one ceases to exist as a human being. However, this definition is still being debated, and some courts have intervened against using this as a definition of death.

The biological definition of death is just one aspect. There are the cultural, social, tribal and psychological dimensions of dealing with lifeless bodies as well.

'Wow, doc!' Harry exclaimed. Just exactly how much have you studied and thought about the definition of death?'

'Well, friend, to serve my patients best, I believe it is mandatory for me to not only learn about extending the quantity and quality of life, but also help them understand the transition between life and the afterlife, respecting whatever beliefs they may have. At the very least, I need to know and understand death, for me to help explain it better. I frequently reflect with my colleagues on how the science of oncology can be seen and learnt in books. But the real-life art of oncology leads one to understand when to stop treatment and shift gears to comfort care—and to prepare the patient for the transition from this body.'

Harry said, 'No wonder Susan believes in you so much!' He paused briefly, then asked in a low voice, as if cautious not to offend my cultural or religious beliefs, 'Do you believe in the afterlife?'

'Yes and no,' I smiled.

'You sound non-committal.'

'Not really, Harry. Once I explain my own set of beliefs, based on a blend of all religious, ritualistic, ethnic, cultural and geographic dimensions, I am sure you will be able to see my perspective. However, for now, I want to stay on the topic at hand.'

'Okay,' Harry agreed. 'Let's stick with the definition of death, as long as you promise to tell me what you think about the afterlife.'

'Deal,' I said. I glanced at my watch to confirm that we still had some time.

'What we've touched upon so far is just the biological and scientific definition of death. However, there are other aspects of death, including cultural, familial, societal and religious ones. Death is not a discrete moment, except in the case of traumatic, accidental or violent death. Most of the time, it is a transition—a process associated with a gradual, visible decline in functionality of the affected individual.'

Prior to the twentieth century, child mortality was sky-high all over the world. Death was a household observation, with brothers and sisters watching their siblings die, parents losing their children, and children losing their friends. It was common to see, touch and feel a dead body. Families and elders used to define death based on personal experience, without a precise definition or criteria as defined in modern societies.

In the post-World War II era, everything about death changed in the Western world. Most communicable diseases became treatable, and increasing longevity meant that a majority of modern Americans would not witness death outside of movies or television shows, most of which involved accidental or traumatic deaths. Along with the change in modes of death, the authority of defining death also shifted, from elders to doctors—and maybe even the judiciary. Remember the famous Terri Schiavo case in the US? In her case, the definition of death went beyond the purview of doctors to the courts! But in most cases today, a person is dead when a doctor declares him dead.

'You are absolutely right, doc,' Harry said, tracking with the history lesson, 'I remember as a child seeing the dead body of my great aunt, who died peacefully at home. Since I moved to the US, I don't recall seeing anyone's mortal remains outside of a funeral home. Why is that?'

'You see, Harry, with the shift in the causality or definition of death, our paradigm has also shifted to planning for death. Often, people in Western society die of old age or chronic illnesses like intractable heart disease or advanced cancer.'

'Like me!' Harry said, conscious of his own finitude.

'Precisely. What I was alluding to was that nowadays there is a possibility of planning for the transition from this life into whatever afterlife one believes he or she is headed towards. Instead of dying from acute infectious epidemics like cholera, plague or flu, many people die in a more predictable fashion. This slow, planned and gradual process also leads to the development of institutions like hospices.'

'Hmmm, now I'm starting to see how you are weaving my own story in with the historical evolution of death,' Harry said. 'You keep bringing up the afterlife, the soul and so on. Please elaborate on it more. How does believing in an afterlife affect one's preparation for death? Is it what shapes the post-death practices? As a Hindu, do you believe in an afterlife too?'

'Harry, your questions are all intelligent and indeed interwoven. I'll try to summarize my answers for you about my thoughts on the afterlife.'

The funeral and last rites we perform for the deceased person should reflect the person's belief system about the afterlife and the existence of the soul. Thus, we care for deceased bodies with respect and give them a proper and graceful farewell. These acts reveal our love and respect for the deceased.

Societies, religions and cultures that regard physical death as a step between two lives, with the passage of the soul into the afterlife, focus on the transition of the deceased into the realm of the dead as the main purpose of the funeral or final rituals. These practices say farewell to the deceased body either through burial or cremation, and rituals and prayers are aimed at enabling the safe passage of the soul—either to unite with the ultimate higher power or to seek new birth. Most of the cultures that believe in the soul-based theory tend to prefer cremation. Evangelical Christians in the US also believe primarily in the soul-based theory but prefer to bury bodies, though some choose cremation. Theologically, they are fine with either.

For religions, cultures and societies that do not believe in the soul-based dualistic existence, the death rituals, as well as the treatment of the corpse, emphasize the separation of the deceased from the realm of the living, and the need for loved ones to cut ties with the dead in a graceful, gradual and gentle fashion. Final rites of passage generally involve the common method of disposing of the body after demise—burial. This has been practised in both the ancient and the modern world, although cremation has slowly been replacing it over the past thirty years or so.

Burial is the most ancient method of disposing of a body. Excavation of ancient sites reveals that Neanderthals and early Homo sapiens were buried. There is also evidence that along with the burial of human remains, our ancestors used to leave behind essential survival items such as tools, food and riches, anticipating that the deceased would carry these along during the transition from this life to the afterlife. This has been seen in some of the oldest burial sites, from the Middle East to northern Europe.

Harry seemed surprised to hear about these ancient burials. 'I thought the most sophisticated treatment for the deceased existed during ancient Egyptian civilization, where pharaohs built massive pyramids to preserve corpses.'

'You're right about the Egyptians,' I said. 'They were among the earliest civilizations known to have cared for their deceased. They developed astonishing and technologically advanced methods of preserving bodies for thousands of years after burying or entombing them. They learnt that the best way to keep the body from decomposing was desiccation.'

'You mean how we use desiccated and dehydrated vegetables and fruits with preserved nutrients? How did they do it? And why? Was it limited to royalty?'

I was pleasantly surprised at how Harry knew his history. 'Egyptians believed that life in human bodies involved three components. First was the physical body, which was a combination of earth, water, fire, space and metals. The second was a universal soul they called "Ka", somewhat equivalent to what many faiths refer to as God. The third was an individual soul, the "Ba", similar to the divine element.

'Upon death, it was believed the "Ka" leaves the body. However, "Ba" remains in close proximity to the mortal remains and visits the deceased body every night to reunite with it.'

I paused, and Harry jumped in to summarize what I had just said.

'So the physical body had to be preserved to allow nightly reunification of the mortal remains and the soul?'

'Correct,' I replied. 'To ensure a smooth entrance to the afterlife, Egyptians developed techniques to desiccate the body, including removal of all organs, except for the heart. This was what is more commonly called mummification. It would allow the body to continue its interaction with the individual soul for thousands of years, according to their beliefs.'

Harry commented, 'This must have been a mammoth task. I think it may have been meant for the privileged class.'

'Not really, Harry. Egyptians have mummified tens of millions of human remains, along with even animals and pets, to facilitate the afterlife! They did not restrict this practice to the royalties or privileged classes.'

'Are you aware of any other ancient civilization doing this?' Harry asked.

I nodded. 'Burial sites in northern Iraq, Israel and northern Europe have revealed some intriguing practices, even before the Egyptians. Some burial sites revealed the evidence of flowers, and even corpses placed in the foetal position in the hope of easier reincarnation. So, as you can see, there have been many variations in the belief of an afterlife and dualistic existence. Even though most cultures that preferred burial did not believe in an afterlife, the historical and archaeological evidence may tell us otherwise.'

'What about cremation? And how do you feel about it?'

Cremation was also an ancient method of disposal of the deceased. Archaeological discovery reveals the evidence of cremation dating back to almost twenty to thirty thousand years. There is evidence of cremation in Australia, ancient Greece and the Roman Empire. In most Eastern countries, like India and Japan, and regions like South Asia, with predominant Hindu and Buddhist culture, cremation was—and still is—the most common post-death ritual.

Europeans preferred burial for almost 1900 years. However, cremation was standard in the ancient Roman Empire until the rise of Christianity. Abrahamic religions—Judaism, Christianity and Islam—believed that cremation involved the desecration of human remains. Eventually, a Christian ruler declared cremation a capital offence. Out of their belief in Christ's resurrection, his followers firmly believed in maintaining bodies as intact as possible. However, during the Great Plague of 1665–66 and the other pandemics of the Middle Ages, in which nearly half of the European population died, mass cremations became common; there was no other way to manage the volume of bodies.

The paradigm gradually shifted due to multiple reasons. To rebel against the conservative approach of traditional church practices, Freemasons started incorporating and approving cremation as a preferred method of post-death ritual among their members. Eventually, it became a necessity due to scarcity of space, combined with more open beliefs towards alternatives to burial. Cremation was officially disapproved by the Catholic Church until 1963, when it was deemed an acceptable alternative to burial. But in some countries with prominent Catholic belief systems, like Italy, cremation is still rare.

As if to make sure he understood, Harry summarized again. 'So, it was not only the culture or one's faith but necessity that determined how we treated our deceased. Tell me, what is involved in cremation and burial? How do they prepare the body? Which method is more environmentally friendly? Are there other more eclectic and eco-friendly ways to dispose of human remains? I can almost start visualizing my mortal remains now!'

Harry's dry chuckle showed that even the sombreness of the discussion couldn't hold down his humour.

Before the Civil War, I told him, the traditional death ritual involved a simple family affair. When a person was deemed nearing death, relatives would go to the terminally ill person's home for the death-watch. Loved ones would visit to bid goodbye and exchange last words with the dying person. This visit also provided support and empathy for the family.

Death was declared by an elder, not by doctors. Once it was decided that a person was dead, family members would wash and care for the body, then make it available for viewing at their home or a church. At a wake or visitation, mourners would gather to express their grief. This was followed by the funeral procession a few days later, where they would transport the corpse from the site of the funeral to the site of the burial.

In contrast, the modern American Christian way of death—which is also shared by Americans following other religions—is characterized by professionalization, medicalization and the industrialization of funeral services. The Civil War resulted in the deaths of nearly a million soldiers. Some of the battlefields and streets were covered with corpses. The families of soldiers who had died on the battlefield wanted to provide final rites to them.

Understanding the severity and critical nature of the challenge, Dr Thomas Holmes developed a system of chemical embalming using arsenic to preserve a body. If a family requested the body of a loved one, it would be embalmed and sent to them so that it could be preserved until the final rites were performed. The profession of 'freelance embalmer' soon arose, and practitioners often set up tents near battlefields to ply their trade.

As the practice of embalming spread, it shaped the funeral industry. Embalming required special facilities, which gave rise to the modern funeral home. The funeral home soon became a place that took care of all the needs of the bereaved. Now, as soon as a person is declared dead by a doctor, the funeral home takes over. The body is transported to the funeral home and, depending on the need for preservation, is embalmed with preservatives and prepared for viewing at the funeral home at a designated time and date.

Once the viewing is completed, depending upon the family's decision, the mortal remains are either buried in a grave or cremated. Cremation of the deceased involves exposing the corpse to extreme heat—1400–1800 degrees Fahrenheit for two to two-and-a-half hours. This reduces it to minerals and bones. In modern cremations, these are then put through a cremulator to reduce them to a granular state. Ashes normally include tiny hard fragments of bone and are handed over to loved ones.

A variation of cremation exists for those who want environmentally friendly cremation. Here the mortician first dissolves the flesh in an alkaline solution, and then, within two hours, grinds down the bones. This is known as flameless cremation. Nearly half of Americans and a majority of northern Europeans who choose cremation opt for this option.

'I think I'd go for flameless cremation,' Harry said. 'Thank you for helping me understand, doc. What about the disposing of the ashes? Can my ashes be scattered over the airfield where I taught people to fly?'

Harry seemed relieved that his first choice was already made.

'Your choice is definitely friendlier to the environment, Harry. With embalming, thousands of tonnes of formaldehyde, a carcinogen, goes into the earth, along with metals and wooden coffins.

'Your desire can be fulfilled, as long as the owners of the property over which your ashes will be scattered agree to it.

In fact, some companies enable you to ship your ashes up into space in low-earth orbit for $5,000, or even outside Earth's orbit for $12,000! You can have your ashes incorporated into a diamond or an old-time vinyl record! Make your choice, my friend. Do you want to hear about any other environmentally friendly options for disposing of your body?'

'I don't think I'll change my mind, but I'd love to hear about them.'

'Well, there's sky burial in parts of the Himalayas.'

'Sky burial?'

'In the Himalayas, extreme cold leaves most of the ground frozen. Burial is impossible. So some Buddhist monks leave the bodies of the deceased for vultures to consume, then collect the residual bones. They believe in returning the elements borrowed from the earth back to nature.'

'Pass,' Harry said, smiling.

'Zoroastrians, the pre-Islamic religion of Iran, preferred to place bodies in what they called the towers of silence, where vultures would consume them.'

'Why so? Environmental reasons?'

'Not exactly. They believed that earth and fire were sacred, and that dead bodies could contaminate both, making burial and cremation both a form of desecration. With their perceived method of funeral, they felt they prevented the tainting of their sacred spaces.'

'Pass,' Harry said, with another grin. 'I prefer the flameless cremation you described. Then dispersing my ashes from my favourite glider at the Bermuda Soaring Club.'

He changed the topic.

'I think I'm now ready to hear the stories of some of your patients. Someone who planned for their funeral while still alive. Not someone like me, at the tail end of life, but someone who was really young and full of life.'

'Sure,' I said. I was happy to go wherever he wanted the conversation to go. 'Let's step inside my office. I want to show you something.'

As we entered my office, my vision clouded as my eyes became moist. This would not be easy.

'See the photo of that beautiful young girl, Harry? Can you see the life flowing from her bright, shining face? Her beautiful smile? Can you see how many dreams she carried for her life that were yet to be fulfilled? Why don't we start with her? Her name is—sorry, her name was—Annie.

'Only her memories are with us now. At the young age of twenty-nine, cancer took away everything she had. Yet, she took control of her own death. She even chose the type of hairstyle she would wear in the coffin, and planned her make-up before she died.'

'Really? Only twenty-eight, and she was planning her own death?'

'Well, my friend, Annie's story is the perfect example of taking control of the process as far as possible. In her case, because of her age, the "why me?" was even more brutal than usual.'

4

Dreams Shattered

To-morrow, to-morrow and to-morrow
Creeps in the petty pace from day to day,
To the last syllable of recorded time:
And all our yesterdays have lighted fools
The way to dusty death. Out, our brief candle!
Life's but a walking shadow, a poor player
That struts and frets his hour upon the stage,
And then is heard no more, it is a tale.
Told by an idiot, full of sound and fury,
Signifying nothing.

—William Shakespeare

Tired from volunteering late at the theatre, Annie awoke to the ringing alarm. She silenced it with a smack and snuggled against Todd's warm back. She sighed, knowing that three unfinished costumes with Friday delivery dates awaited her at work and Jess wasn't scheduled to return for another two weeks.

As Annie moved to a sitting position, every muscle in her body screamed in protest. She rolled her shoulders and felt a pain in her right breast. Maybe she'd pulled a muscle. The lighting and camera equipment she had moved last night was heavy, but she had moved it before without injury or muscle aches the following day.

With a deep yawn, Annie climbed out of bed and made her way to the bathroom. She flicked on the light and removed her nightshirt. In addition to the tenderness, her right breast had a new red and swollen area on the outside of her nipple. Worry picked at her mind as she outlined the swelling with her fingertips. Her back and shoulder muscles were stiff and sore from exertion, but the feeling in her breast was different.

The warm shower improved the muscle stiffness in her body but had no effect on her breast. Annie pushed the discomfort to the back of her mind. Breast tissue was more sensitive than back muscles. Perhaps it required additional healing time.

After slipping into jeans and a T-shirt, she ran a brush through the long, dark hair that tickled her hip, then braided it into a thick rope gathered at the nape of her neck. With every movement, the discomfort in her right breast caused her to wince. She flipped off the light. The rent was due in two weeks. If nothing unexpected came up, maybe she could afford a clinic visit after she sent the landlord the monthly cheque. Annie slipped out of the front door to avoid disturbing Todd. For now, she had to finish those costumes.

For the rest of the week, Annie immersed herself in meeting her deadline. As she selected sequins, scarves and fabrics, the art consumed her—until every time she had to raise her right arm. The soreness in her breast was not improving.

Over the next few days, analgesics became part of her diet. During the day, she focused on her work. Sleeping presented a challenge. With nothing to occupy her mind, the tenderness seemed to intensify. The day Annie mailed the rent, she left work for a quick appointment at the local urgent care centre.

A middle-aged physician dressed in a white lab coat entered the examining room, holding a clipboard. 'Ms Carlson, I'm Dr Smith. Tell me about the problem.'

'A few days ago, when I woke up, it was swollen and red. It hurts every time I move my shoulder. I take aspirin, but it doesn't help much.'

Although the physician didn't apply a lot of pressure as he palpated the swelling, Annie had to grit her teeth to keep from crying out. His deep frown of concentration made her nervous. Maybe it wasn't just a pulled muscle.

'You have a lot of inflammation in the tissue. How long has this been going on?'

Annie concentrated on the past few weeks. 'Sorry, it wasn't just a few days. It's been almost two weeks. I've been so busy. I guess time got away from me. I noticed it the day after I set up the theatre audiovisual equipment. Occasionally, I lift heavy equipment, so I thought I'd pulled something.'

'Do you remember any specific incident in which you may have injured yourself?'

Since Annie had spent a lot of time in the theatre, she was adept at reading non-verbal cues. Dr Smith's facial expression and tone didn't match the nonchalant way he tried to phrase his question. As she recalled the night before she noticed the problem, her heart rate accelerated, and she could feel the perspiration on her upper lip.

'I don't remember anything,' she answered.

'You could have suffered a minor trauma or injury. Sometimes an infection, a condition called mastitis or inflammation of the breast, results after an injury. There may be a small abscess forming. I'll write you a prescription for antibiotics. You need to return in two weeks. If we don't get adequate response on this, we may need to schedule additional testing.'

Annie exhaled in relief. Just an infection. In a few days, she'd be good as new.

As with many artists, Annie Carlson had struggled with the transition from education to employment. After completing her studies in New York and multiple relocations, she and her husband, Todd, had finally settled in Phoenix, Arizona. Although a native of South Carolina, Annie felt comfortable in her new home. She hadn't attained all of her personal goals yet, but she was close.

Money was in short supply, but she had found a fantastic job designing costumes for Broadway shows and theatre artistes. At this stage in her life, she refused to worry about multiple shifts and the lack of healthcare coverage. She and Todd were young and healthy, and they would improve their earning potential and benefits as time passed.

At home, Annie placed her antibiotic bottle near the kitchen sink and diligently adhered to the prescribed schedule. Every morning in the shower, she checked her breast. Gradually, the swelling slowly subsided and the tenderness improved. After two weeks, her breast was no longer sore, but it still didn't look like her left breast. The doctor had told her to return if things didn't improve. Annie checked her side-view reflection. He had said 'improve', and she had improved. She just needed more time to heal because she worked so much. Her mum had always harped on about her work schedule, and perhaps she was right. However, Annie couldn't afford to cut back yet. Things would chill in a few more weeks. As soon as she had a lull in her schedule, she would get another appointment if her breast wasn't totally healed.

Again, life and work occupied Annie's thoughts and time. The Arizona desert moved into summer and temperatures soared. One day, as Annie slid behind the steering wheel for the short commute home, perspiration beaded her collarbone and trickled down her cleavage. Even that caused pain to slice through her right breast. As she rolled down the window to let in some air,

Annie repositioned her right arm to alleviate the discomfort. Over the past week, she had ignored the returning pain. Today, it was different. At first, it had been localized in a spot near her nipple. Now her entire right breast seemed on fire.

The following day, Annie left work early for an appointment with Dr Smith. Tension tightened her shoulders as she thumbed through a magazine in the waiting room. The office visit and more antibiotics would take a big bite from her next paycheque. What would she do if he ordered additional testing?

'Think positive,' she scolded herself.

The nurse called her name, and Dr Smith entered the exam room eight minutes later. 'Ms Carlson, looks like your abscess is back.'

Annie nodded and gritted her teeth as he gently palpated her inflamed right breast.

'Last time, we caught it when it was forming. This time it looks like it's a full-blown abscess.'

While Annie dressed, he wrote another prescription. 'I'm ordering an ultrasound so we can determine the size and location of the problem. After a week of antibiotic therapy, I want you to have a biopsy.'

Two thoughts hit Annie—how much would it cost, and how much would it hurt? Her breast was well beyond tender, and she'd already endured two exams. Worse, another visit would consume the small amount of extra income she would take home from this week's paycheque.

Financial concerns clouded Annie's thoughts until a young woman almost Annie's age entered the ultrasound room. 'Hi, my name's Marcie. I'm the ultrasound technician.'

The tension in Annie's stomach eased. Marcie had small, capable hands and a gentle voice. Maybe it wouldn't be too bad.

'This may feel a little cold,' Marcie said as she squeezed some thick jelly over Annie's breast.

Prepared for pain, Annie balled her hands into fists. Marcie moved a round, smooth probe over Annie's swollen breast. Annie relaxed her fingers. Although the light pressure was uncomfortable, the jelly allowed the probe to glide over the skin and reduce the pain. Once certain she could manage the physical discomfort, she turned her attention to the wavy patterns on the black-and-white screen.

Marcie paused and pressed the intercom. 'Dr Sharp, can you come to the ultrasound room?'

Annie's gaze flicked from the screen to Marcie. Was her technician new at this procedure and needed some help, or was something abnormal showing up on the screen?

The radiologist, Dr Sharp, arrived and, after a cursory introduction, peered at the screen. Marcie outlined a dark spot in the middle of a bunch of wavy lines. Annie swallowed past the lump in her throat. Although she had never met the radiologist, something was going on, and she could tell it would be bad news and would cost more money than she had.

'Is there someone with you today?' he asked.

'No. I came alone. Why?'

'I want to perform a needle biopsy to obtain a tissue sample. I don't like the look of this spot.' Again, he indicated the dark shadow on the screen. 'If I do this today, we can get a diagnosis right away.'

Although dollar signs flashed through her mind, Annie wanted to get the procedure behind her and move on with her life. 'How long will it take?'

'Twenty minutes—not for the procedure. A biopsy only takes a few minutes. We like patients to stay after the procedure to ensure they're feeling okay.'

Annie tried to concentrate on the conversation, but the word 'biopsy' started rattling her mind. Where else had she heard it? Hadn't Aunt Martha had a biopsy? Fear made her heart race in her chest. Aunt Martha's biopsy had preceded her cancer diagnosis and the horrors of chemotherapy and radiation. However, Aunt Martha was much older than Annie, who was only twenty-nine.

'Ms Carlson?'

Annie came back to the present. 'The biopsy, right? Let's get it over with.'

Except for the prick from the local anaesthetic, the biopsy led to little physical pain. However, it was the mental stress that pushed Annie to the edge. During the procedure, she played the what-if game. What were the chances someone her age could get breast cancer? Would they have to remove her breast? How would Todd react if she was scarred from the procedure?

As she dressed following the biopsy, Annie adjusted her bra to alleviate the pressure on her tender breast and the small surgical site. She lifted her blouse and hesitated. Todd? Should she tell him about the biopsy or wait a few days until she had the results? She fastened the buttons of her shirt and picked up her handbag. This news would make him crazy with worry, and it was going to be needless anyway, right?

But by the time she parked the car in front of the apartment, she felt like she had slowly unravelled and was hanging on by a mere thread. Todd wasn't due to arrive home from work for another three hours. In the meantime, Annie unlocked the door and walked to the wall phone.

After three rings, the line connected to her mother, Jill, in South Carolina.

'Hey, Mum.'

'Annie, I was just thinking about you. How is your breast infection?'

'I'm much better. I saw the doctor today, and the infection cleared up. A radiologist took a biopsy to make sure everything was okay.'

Silence filled the line.

'Biopsy?' Jill's voice trembled.

'Wait, Mum. I don't want to scare you. They just did it because I kept getting breast infections. The doctor's going to call in a couple of days with the results. I'm sure it's going to be fine.'

'You let me know as soon as you hear from him,' Jill said.

Annie could tell by her mum's voice that she was having a hard time processing the information, and if she was honest with herself, Annie felt the same way. It was just too much for both of them right now.

'I've got to start cooking dinner. Todd will be home soon,' Annie said, infusing her voice with a cheerfulness she didn't feel.

'Call me the minute you find out, okay?'

'I will, promise.'

The call from Dr Smith came while Annie and Todd were working. Since Annie arrived home first, she played the message. Dr Smith didn't indicate the biopsy results in the message. He requested that she come to the office as soon as possible. Annie pressed the play button for the third time and slumped into the worn dinette chair. It had to be bad news. Why else would he ask her to come in as soon as possible?

When Todd arrived thirty minutes later, she plastered a smile on her face, but Todd wasn't to be fooled. He took one look at her and his cheerful expression faded. 'Annie?'

Annie threw her arms around his neck. 'I'm so scared.'

Tenderly, he unfolded her arms and held her hands in his. He searched her face as if he could read her thoughts. 'Is it the biopsy results?'

Annie nodded. 'Dr Smith left a message to come to his office as soon as possible.'

Todd folded her back into an embrace. 'We'll go first thing in the morning.'

Annie and Todd entered the stucco office building hand in hand. After signing in, Annie picked up a magazine from the small oak end table but didn't have a chance to open the pages. The nurse called her name, and they both followed the young woman to Dr Smith's private office. He joined them within moments.

Annie studied the physician's lined forehead as he shook hands with Todd and then pulled up a chair in front of them. His gaze travelled from Todd to Annie, and he said, 'I'm sorry. I have bad news. Your biopsy shows you have a very aggressive form of breast cancer.'

Although the physician continued to talk, Annie's thoughts hit a wall the moment the word 'cancer' entered her ears. Memories roiled through her mind with one consistent thought: 'Am I going to die? What about Todd? What about the family we will never have? What about the house we will never purchase?'

Todd said, 'Are you sure? She's so young. Maybe the pathologist made a mistake—got her test confused with someone else's.'

Annie struggled to concentrate on Dr Smith's response.

'I know this is hard to hear, but we double-check the results. Also, the biopsy results confirm my physical findings. Annie has a large tumour. The weight and volume have disfigured her breast. It's warm and extremely tender to touch. When you feel it, it's like a rock embedded in soft tissue.'

Annie pressed her fingers to her right temple, careful not to touch her arm against her chest. Everything Dr Smith said was true. What were they going to do? They didn't have insurance. Their savings were almost non-existent.

Twenty minutes after they had arrived, Annie and Todd stepped outside into a new world. The sun didn't appear as bright, but the heat seemed stifling. Annie felt as if she couldn't breathe. She had breast cancer. If she still had a life ahead of her, she knew it would never be the same.

Todd drove back to the apartment without saying a word. Annie glanced at him as they walked to the apartment door.

She'd never seen his features appear so void of emotion. He had to be in shock because Todd's sensitivity to people and his environment was what had drawn Annie to him in the first place. That trait was also the reason Annie held her tears at bay.

The moment Todd closed the door behind them, he embraced her. She squeezed her eyes closed, trying to suppress the tears. It felt as if the walls of her world were closing in, and she was trapped inside them. She struggled for breath and then forced her mouth to form the words, 'It's all over.'

'No. It can't be. I won't let it,' Todd whispered in a ragged voice that Annie had never heard before.

'I wish you had that kind of power. I wish I could erase this— all of this horror.'

Todd broke the embrace, holding her upper arms in his strong hands. 'It could still be a mistake. I read an article about . . .'

'It's not a mistake. It's big, and it's growing every day. That's why Dr Smith wants me to start treatment as soon as possible.'

'So you'll get the treatment and then you'll be cured, right?'

Annie shook her head. 'We don't have health insurance and we're almost broke.'

'Don't worry about the money. That's the least of our worries. We'll get what we need. I don't care what it takes. We'll get what we need to get you well. You're young and strong. You can beat this.'

Annie pressed her fist to her lips but couldn't stop the tears. 'I don't know.'

Todd's features always displayed his feelings. Right now, the panic and fear Annie read in the tremble of his chin almost broke her heart. He swallowed once, but the desperate attempt did nothing to quell the storm brewing inside. He pulled her against him and wept into the hollow of her neck. Sobs racked his wide shoulders.

Ignoring the discomfort in her breast, Annie hugged him close. 'I'm sorry,' she whispered.

'Say you'll get better,' Todd pleaded.

'I can't. It's bad, honey. It's really bad.'

'No, Annie. I can't lose you. You're my life.'

Annie's iron will dissolved into tears. Together, they cried for their lost life. They cried in fear of the unknown. They cried in desperation.

With swollen eyes and a sniffle, Todd finally released her. 'What are we going to do?'

Annie shook her head. 'I don't know. I can't even think. I just feel numb.'

Todd pulled a tissue from the dispenser on the counter and blew his nose. 'We won't give up, Annie. Not you and me. We won't give up.'

'I love you,' she whispered.

'I love you too,' Todd said. 'But I can't think about this any more. Do you want to take a walk?'

Annie glanced at the fading light through the front window. The apartment complex had a nice walking path. When they'd first moved in, they couldn't get enough of desert walks. Annie glanced at the horizon, but the desert didn't call to her as it usually did.

'I don't feel like it right now. Besides, I need to call Mum.'

Todd pulled on his ball cap. 'I've got to get some air.'

'Go ahead. I'll talk to Mum while you're gone.'

Todd paused with his hand on the door. 'Are you sure you're ready to talk about it?'

Annie shook her head but picked up the phone. 'No, but I need to tell Mum what's going on.'

As the soft creaking of the front door announced Todd's departure, silence filled the apartment. For the first time in her life, Annie felt truly alone. She loved Todd and was certain of his love for her, but this was cancer. Cancer. He didn't know—couldn't know—how it felt to be . . . dying. Like a long-starved desert plant praying for rain, Annie grasped for the one person who had always been there for her. A tear slid down her cheek as she entered her mother's phone number into the hand unit.

'Hello?' Mum's voice filtered through the receiver moments later.

At the sound of the familiar voice, Annie's tears started again. 'Mum, it's me.'

'Honey, what's wrong? You don't sound like yourself.'

'I—I have cancer, and I don't know what to do.'

'Oh, dear God, no!'

Only moments ago, Annie was certain she'd cried every last tear she had in her, but the distress in her mum's voice opened the floodgates all over again.

As suddenly as they had started, her mum's soft sobs stopped. 'Annie, listen to me. We'll get through this. I want you and Todd to take the next available flight to Charlotte. Do you have enough money for tickets?'

'We can't just leave. We have jobs, responsibilities.'

'You have a responsibility to yourself first,' her mother said firmly. 'Do you have enough money for a flight home?'

'I think so.'

'Do I need to come out there and help you get ready to leave? I can do that if you need me to.'

Annie wiped her face with a tissue. 'No, I can manage.'

'Be strong, sweetheart. We'll deal with this together. I love you, and I'll always be here for you, okay?'

'Okay.'

'Call me back as soon as you book your flight.' Her mother continued to talk, but Annie felt as if she were in a surreal dream world. There were sounds coming through the phone, but nothing made sense.

'Annie?'

'Mum?'

'Honey, let me make the airline reservations for you.'

'No. I can do it. I have to talk to Todd,' Annie said, struggling to clear the fog of confusion in her mind.

'Do you know his schedule this week?'

Annie sniffed. 'Mum, I can't think. Everything's so messed up.'

'I know. Just come home. I'll help you. We'll get through this together, as a family, just like we have in the past for everything. Okay?'

'Okay.'

'Take one step at a time. All you need to do is get Todd's schedule and call me. I'll find a flight for you. Can you do that?'

They said goodbye and Annie pressed the 'end' key and placed the receiver on the counter. She pressed her fingers against her temples. Think. She wasn't the only woman to have been diagnosed with breast cancer. She'd read of others who had survived, hadn't she? Then the memory of Aunt Martha sent a shiver down her spine. Cancer had claimed Aunt Martha's life after a long, miserable battle.

Annie stroked a strand of hair tickling her temple. Aunt Martha had not only lost all of her hair, she'd also suffered through weeks of nausea and vomiting before her death. Annie dropped into the kitchen chair and held her head in her hands. Airline reservations. She needed to check times. Her fingers stumbled over the keys of her laptop, but after a few attempts, she opened the airline website. Several flights left for Charlotte every day, but the red-eye was the cheapest.

The absurdity of the situation nearly made her laugh. Tickets to Charlotte were a drop in the bucket compared to cancer treatment. How would they pay for it? Would she need surgery? She printed out the available flights and exited the site.

Annie pulled her worn travel bag from the closet shelf and opened it on the bed. She'd hoped to one day save the money for a weekend getaway with Todd, but this wasn't the getaway she had in mind. She folded her favourite tie cardigan. Why had she and Todd let money and work stop them from enjoying quality time together? Until today, she'd never resented the personal delays. Annie added underwear to her bag. Now she wondered about her decision to postpone the important things—details she had taken for granted.

As she selected shoes and tucked them into the sides of her bag, she ticked off the postponed dreams. She and Todd would take more time together, later. She and Todd would have money for a down payment on a house, later. She and Todd would start a family, later. Now she wondered if she would ever have a later. All those sacrifices, time wasted, time she didn't have. Had her life clock already started ticking and she'd been too busy with unimportant tasks to notice?

In the tiny bathroom, Annie placed her toiletries and extra hairbands on the counter. She glanced at the mirror and didn't recognize her reflection. The haunted image in the mirror escalated her fear. Annie touched the dark strand of hair at her temple. She'd always believed her hair was one of her best assets and she had never cut it. Would she need chemotherapy? Would her hair fall out by the handfuls, as Aunt Martha's had? Todd liked the way the dark waves snaked around her nude body when they made love. Would she ever do that again?

Annie stomped her foot against the vinyl floor. No! The cancer was a big mistake and as soon as she returned to Charlotte, the doctors would confirm it. Only older women like her aunt died of cancer. Discomfort pulled her gaze to her chest. Even beneath the silky fabric of her bra, her breast ached with heat and swelling. But still . . . she couldn't be dying?

With a hard jerk that rattled the glass near the sink, Annie opened the cabinet drawer and snatched her toothbrush and the tube of paste. Had her vanity caused this? She'd gladly trade her life for her hair.

'I'll cut it and use it for a wig for myself and sell the rest,' she promised herself. 'Just let me get my life back.'

Annie pitched her comb and brush into the toiletry bag. She was the star in a nightmare and there wasn't a chance she'd wake up. Wake up? She might not even live long enough to witness the ending.

Just last week her friends and colleagues had laughed at the black balloons and tombstone decor she had picked out for her thirtieth birthday. It was the death of her adolescence, after all. This week, though, it looked like thirty might be her last birthday ever.

The next morning, as the sun climbed the horizon and brought a pink tint into the bedroom, Annie stretched and snuggled against the warmth of Todd's back. Her eyes were burning and swollen from hours of crying. Yesterday's events crowded her thoughts. It wasn't a bad dream. She had cancer. She might be dying. However, she wasn't going to fold like one of those inexpensive chairs she always hated stacking backstage. Within thirty minutes of Todd coming home from his walk, Annie had completed the reservations for their trip to Charlotte on tonight's red-eye.

In South Carolina, Annie's mother checked the guest bedroom again. When Annie had married and moved to Phoenix, it had taken several months for Jill to adjust to the absence of her daughter. However, that touch of the empty-nest syndrome couldn't compete with the feeling of loss overwhelming her now. She wasn't going to just be separated by a few miles. If Annie couldn't be cured, Jill might lose her.

Jill searched through her pants pocket for a tissue. As she wiped the trickle of tears down her cheeks, she vowed she'd control her emotions. Annie didn't need a weeping willow—she needed an oak. Jill had to be strong, and she had to help Annie be strong in her fight against cancer.

With renewed determination, Jill closed the door to block out the photos of Annie on her first bike, Annie at graduation, and Annie and Todd's wedding. Jill drew strength by moving forward, not by looking back. Last night she had gathered her husband and Annie's younger brother around her. They had wept together. However, after the tears, they had garnered family strength and made a simple plan to help Annie. As the matriarch, Jill shouldered the primary responsibility.

'Stay strong,' she repeated to herself as she checked her purse for her keys.

At the Charlotte airport, Jill parked and hurried to the passenger-arrival area. According to the monitor, Todd and Annie's flight had landed and passengers would be disembarking within minutes. Jill located an empty seat and waited. She had contacted Jodie, one of her friends, about a good oncologist. Jodie hadn't hesitated. She had recently lost her father to cancer. She had been to our clinic multiple times and had witnessed first-hand our philosophy of care. She directed Jill to my office. It was also conveniently close to Jill's home.

Jill squeezed her eyes shut to suppress her tears. She couldn't think of beautiful Annie as a cancer patient. 'Be strong,' she whispered to herself again.

As she scanned the faces of passengers on the escalator, a wave drew her focus. She blinked. Annie waved again, but she wasn't smiling. Todd wore a stoic half-smile. At the bottom of the escalator, Annie hurried forward.

Jill hugged her close, and Annie sobbed into her shoulder. Jill's 'be strong' mantra evaporated in tears. Annie was too young and vibrant. Cancer should have struck Jill instead. She had lived her life and raised a family. Her beautiful Annie was just getting started.

Jill rubbed Annie's back just as she had when Annie was little. 'Don't cry. We're going to get through this.'

'I'm scared, Mum.'

'I know, honey. I am too. But we're here, together. I found a doctor who specializes in cancer treatment. He'll see you if it's okay with you.'

Annie massaged her forehead. 'Does he know we don't have insurance?'

'Yes.'

Todd directed them to the baggage claim. 'I don't care who she sees as long as she goes right away.'

As soon as Jill had settled Todd and Annie into the guest room, she called my office and made an appointment for Annie. Heartsick, she then busied herself preparing the family meal. Although she understood she couldn't protect Annie from the disease eating at her body, she could still prepare a healthy meal, provide shelter and give her daughter a mother's love and support.

The dinner conversation covered everything but health. Everyone worked hard to act as if Annie was healthy, and the family gathering was merely an unexpected visit. But this was no visit. This was a family in crisis.

The following morning, Jill drove them to my office. The stucco building with the brick interface that housed Carolina Blood and Cancer Care Associates was located only a few blocks from the local hospital. Todd held Annie's hand as they entered through the double glass doors. Inside, another patient waited in the reception area, watching the flat screen mounted to the wall with unseeing eyes. Todd and Annie selected a seat near the large fish tank while Jill gave Annie's name to the receptionist. Within minutes, a young woman with a smile as bright as her royal purple scrubs appeared in the doorway and called Annie's name.

'We'd like to accompany her,' Jill said.

'No problem. My name is Debbie. Annie, I need to weigh you before I take you to the examining room.'

After checking her height and weight, Debbie took her into the waiting room and was taking Annie's blood pressure when I walked in.

'Hello, I'm Dr Patel. How can I help you?'

Jill noted the immediate panic in her daughter's eyes and responded instead.

'My daughter, Annie, flew in last night. Her doctor in Phoenix just diagnosed her with breast cancer and said she needed treatment right away.'

'I'll be happy to help in any way I can. Do you want me to continue with treatment until you return to Phoenix?'

Jill waited a beat to see if Todd or Annie wanted to take over the conversation. When they didn't respond, she said, 'Annie and Todd have moved back to Rock Hill so they can be with family. They don't have health insurance.'

'Let's work on treatment first. We can work out financial matters later. Did you bring your records from Phoenix?'

Annie shook her head.

I gave her a reassuring smile. 'If you give me your doctor's name, my staff will call and get everything we need. I'd like to examine you first, and then we can discuss the best treatment for you.'

Jill's shoulders slumped as she left the room with Todd. This was still the easy part. Right now, I was examining her baby—her only daughter. Would my findings be better? Worse?

Within ten minutes, Annie and I joined Todd and Jill in my office. 'I feel we are dealing with a serious situation,' I told them. 'Annie's tumour is very large. I also felt the lymph nodes under her arm. This means the cancer may already have metastasized or travelled to her lymph system. When I pressed on this area, I felt swelling. This fluid build-up is caused when the cancer tissue liquefies.'

Obviously frightened by the explanation, Jill glanced at Annie and Todd. They stared at me with blank expressions. Jill picked up her pen and scribbled my description with a trembling hand. She couldn't let herself slide into terror. She needed to be strong so she could help Annie understand her disease after the shock subsided.

Once I finished explaining, Jill swallowed past a bone-dry throat and asked, 'How do we treat this?'

'We need to consult with a surgeon to biopsy one of the lymph nodes as well as drain some of the fluid from the axilla.'

'Do you know a surgeon who will take Annie's case . . . even without insurance?'

'Absolutely! Please, you have enough worries. Let me help you with the arrangements.'

Jill exhaled as at least the financial burden lifted. 'Thank you. Will Annie have to stay in hospital?'

'No, I think we can do this on an outpatient basis. Once we get the biopsy results, we will talk again about the best course of treatment.'

Jill squeezed Annie's hand. 'Honey, do you have questions?'

Annie shook her head.

I said, 'This type of cancer is unusual for your age. Did anyone in your family have breast cancer?'

The question seemed to pull Annie out of her shock-induced confusion. She pushed back a long, dark tendril of hair that had drifted near her right eye. 'My aunt had ovarian cancer. She died at forty-seven.'

I responded, 'I don't want to lose any more time. My nurse will draw blood for some tests, and I will arrange for what we call CAT scans at the hospital. Don't worry, a scan doesn't hurt. It's like a fancy X-ray that tells us if the cancer has metastasized to any other area of the body. The answers from these tests will help me determine the best course of treatment.

'After that, we'll talk to several non-profit foundations to help coordinate payment. Our business officer will work with you so finances don't create more stress.'

Within five minutes, we had made an appointment with a surgeon and scheduled the scans at the adjacent hospital. I handed Annie a card with the appointment times written on the back. 'I want to see you next week. If you have any questions before then, feel free to call me.'

With cancer, Annie had entered a hurry-up-and-wait mode. While I had arranged an immediate appointment with the surgeon, she would still have to wait for the results. The CT scans were completed immediately, but she had to wait for the radiologist to review them. The waiting was by far more dreadful than any of the procedures.

On the day of her follow-up appointment with me, Annie didn't know if she wanted to throw up or hide, but she would at least have some clarity after the appointment. She could fight the invader in her body better if she understood the battle looming before her. She had spent a week waiting, worrying and crying. But now, it was time to stand tall and move to action.

I met Annie, Jill and Todd in my private office. Outside the office window, the birds chirped and the sun bathed the grass golden. Inside, perspiration bathed Annie's sides in spite of the cool air pumping through the air-conditioned building. Now that the time had arrived, she wasn't sure she wanted to know the information in the folder in my hands.

'Annie, the tumour in your breast measures 4.5x5 inches. According to the biopsy report, the cancer has spread to the lymph nodes in the axilla and we also found malignant cells in the fluid Dr Jevel drained from your arm. This makes your cancer a stage 3B. However, it hasn't spread to your bones or other tissue— and this is encouraging. There is a small but definite chance that we can shrink your tumour with treatment.'

Annie sucked in her breath to maintain her calm. Okay, she could deal with this. Based on what I had told her during her first exam, she had suspected the node in her underarm would be positive. The good news was that it hadn't spread to other parts of her body.

'Okay,' she said.

'Dr Jevel recommends that we start treatment to shrink your tumour before he removes it. I agree.'

Annie had prepared for her visit in advance, so questions were fresh in her mind. 'Can you be more specific? I need to understand the kind of treatment, how long it will last, what to expect if you think I need more than one kind, and the side effects.'

During her first visit, Annie had been in fear and shock. Fear still plagued her, but it no longer paralysed her. She'd told her mum and Todd that she wasn't going to shrivel up and die without a fight. A fight meant she had to take responsibility for her decisions and her life. She was glad Jill and Todd were there for support, but they didn't have cancer. She did. She focused on the conversation with me.

'I'm glad you're asking so many questions,' I said. 'I expect them from my patients, and I'll do my best to share as much information as I can about where we go from here. Keep in mind that each patient is unique, so the treatment course, side effects and outcomes will vary. I'll always be honest with you. If I feel we aren't getting the expected response, I'll tell you so we can discuss your options.'

'I appreciate that,' Annie said.

'I'm here to help you through this journey in every possible way, but I'm not God and I don't have a crystal ball.'

Annie closed her eyes, acknowledging the unspoken message. She understood that some people survived cancer and others did not. She planned to do everything she could to be a survivor.

'We will start with two chemicals—Adriamycin and Cytoxan. Both chemicals are cell poisons and attack your cancer cells at different stages of multiplication. We give four doses of both every three weeks. The drugs can cause nausea, vomiting, alopecia and low blood count, but we will take precautions to minimize these negative effects.'

I paused and looked at the beautiful hair framing her face like tiny silk threads. Annie touched her hair. It would fall out and I was reluctant to tell her. 'I'm sorry,' I said. 'Alopecia means hair loss. I can't give you anything to prevent that.'

Annie clenched her jaw as I confirmed her suspicions. Her hair was the least of her concerns. Right now she was more concerned with living.

The Friday before the Labor Day holiday, Annie marched into our chemotherapy treatment room. In her life before cancer, Annie would have loved the room with its large navy easy chairs facing a long bank of windows opening out to the garden. In her new life after her cancer diagnosis, she recognized that the garden helped patients relax and meditate or pray for strength to fight the battle inside their bodies. However, increased cancer treatment knowledge wasn't the only thing that had changed for Annie. Last year, she had looked forward to the Labor Day holiday away from work. Now, long weekends and holidays meant nothing. Cancer wouldn't take a break because it was Labor Day.

As Debbie motioned towards a chair, Annie squared her shoulders. Her career struggles had taught her the valuable lesson of tenacity. In the big scheme of things, her work in theatre was peanuts compared to a cancer diagnosis, but she knew how to dig in and stay the course. Now she had a new job—fighting for her life. She was ready for the challenge.

Debby rolled in a small cart beside the chair with tubing, tape and multiple small- and medium-sized bags of fluid. Annie winced as Debbie inserted the needle into her arm.

'The larger bag is just fluids to help keep the line open so we can infuse the important drugs,' Debby explained as she picked up a plastic bag about the size of a sandwich. 'This bag contains the medicine to help prevent nausea and vomiting.'

Although Annie had read about her treatment plan and I had explained the actions of the drugs and their side effects, anxiety still clawed at her belly. They were going to infuse her with poison. It was supposed to kill mainly cancer cells, but it was still poison. To hold her fear at bay, Annie focused on the little bag as it dripped into her vein. Lots of folks used the anti-emetics she was being given. With any luck, they would keep her from getting sick.

Debby waited for the anti-emetic drugs to complete, then picked up a syringe. 'This one burns, but it won't last long,' she told Annie.

With a quick turn of her wrist, Debby attached the syringe to the tubing connected to Annie's arm and slowly pushed in the plunger. The red liquid moved towards the cannula taped to Annie's arm. Within seconds liquid fire engulfed her flesh.

'It won't last long. It won't last long. It won't last long,' Annie chanted silently through gritted teeth.

When the burning stopped, she exhaled.

An hour later, Debby detached the empty bags and removed the cannula from Annie's arm. Annie breathed in deeply, then exhaled slowly. The treatment was over.

'That's it. Unless you have a problem, we'll see you in three weeks. Don't forget to drink lots of fluids,' Debby said.

'I will. Thanks.'

Annie refused to sit idly and worry. She dug in and researched her disease. By the time she received her second treatment, she had replaced fear with hope. She believed the chemo was shrinking her tumour. Every time she visited the surgeon, he drained a smaller quantity of fluid from around the tumour.

After a month of chemo, Annie's hair started to fall out. But instead of grieving her loss, she faced it with a positive attitude.

Some days the loss of her beautiful hair got to her, but for the most part, she kept a smile on her face and hope in her heart. Every time she removed a clump of hair from her brush, she imagined the chemotherapy shrinking her tumour.

Annie made an appointment with Jodie, a hair stylist who was one of her mother's best friends, to shave off the rest of her hair. She was going to lose it anyway.

Shortly after she received her buzz cut, Annie's surgeon reported that her fluid build-up had stopped, so she wouldn't have to return until she'd completed her four doses of chemotherapy. Annie pumped her fist. She'd won another skirmish. Now she'd carry on until her last dose. As soon as the chemotherapy ended, Dr Jevel would reassess her tumour. If the mass had shrivelled and released its tentacles from her chest wall, Dr Jevel could surgically remove it. With this information, Annie walked a tightrope. She didn't look forward to surgery, but she longed for the reassurance that her tumour had been excised from her body.

'Don't expect too much too soon,' she told herself.

Cancer had taught her an important lesson: When you don't know how many days remain, don't wish your life away. Easy to say, hard to live out. How do you maintain hope without aiming so high that the fall breaks you?

On Halloween, Annie reported to the clinic for her final dose of chemotherapy. She settled into the recliner and focused on the calming qualities of the garden. Although the last of the summer plants had started withering before our short South Carolina winter, Annie looked for signs of life. Beside her, Debby prepared to inject the Adriamycin that Annie referred to as 'red poison'. Outside the window, a tiny hummingbird with a bright red throat and a small, hairless patch on its head sucked nectar from a feeder.

'You also drink the bright red nectar. Do you suffer from breast cancer?' she whispered to the tiny bird.

A larger hummingbird darted at the smaller bird, but it held its position, its tiny wings beating so quickly that only a blur was visible.

Annie smiled in spite of the fire streaking up her arm. 'Check out that hummingbird. This must be her third dose of chemo too.'

'Chemo?' Debby said as she turned towards the window.

'Yeah, see how the feathers on her head are gone and she's drinking red poison just like you injected in my arm?'

Debby's laugh filled the quiet area. 'Works for me!'

Annie kept the smile frozen on her face. An hour later, she had reached the end of her chemo journey. But would it be enough to kill the tumour?

A few days later, at Dr Jevel's office, Annie waited with apprehension. Her life had filtered down to the information the surgeon would provide. Would it be good news, bad news or just okay news?

When the office staff called her name, she stood and whispered, 'Good news, please.'

The nurse escorted her to the surgeon's office, where Dr Jevel joined her five minutes later. She read his tentative smile and swallowed. He wasn't going to deliver the news she'd hoped for.

Dr Jevel levered his hip on to the edge of his desk and flipped a page in her file. 'Well, Annie, the tumour has responded to the chemotherapy, but not as much as we'd hoped.'

Although she maintained her smile, her heart accelerated right after the word 'but'. 'What's that mean?'

'Your tumour has decreased by almost a third. That's really encouraging and means your cancer cells are sensitive to the drugs you've been given. However, there's still a sizable tumour in your breast and it hasn't pulled free of your chest wall. I think if we give you another round of chemo, it will shrink to a size I can remove. When I go in, I want to have the best chance at removing all of it.'

Disappointed, Annie and her mother returned home. How would her body react to another round of chemo? Although it hadn't been the nightmare she'd anticipated, she didn't relish the thought of another round.

Outside her bedroom window, grey clouds darkened the afternoon sun. The bright reds and yellows of fall had faded to browns. Life outside had gone dormant. If the next round of chemo didn't work, was she also moving into the winter of her life?

Her mother found Annie staring out the bedroom window and wrapped her arm around her daughter's shoulders. 'I know you're disappointed, but at least your tumour responded,' Jill said.

Annie hid her worry behind a bright smile. Mum had been through a lot, and she didn't want to worry her more. 'You're right. By spring, I'll be good to go.'

One week before Thanksgiving, Annie reported to our clinic for her second round of chemotherapy. She had given herself a pep talk, so, as she pushed through the glass-door entrance, there was a smile on her face and a spring to her step.

The first time around, she'd adjusted to the cherry-red Adriamycin firing through her veins. Today, the Adriamycin had been replaced with another powerful drug called docetaxel. She sank into her favourite treatment chair and breathed deeply.

I had told her that patients typically suffered fewer side effects from docetaxel. As Debby approached with the bags of solution, Annie took another deep breath. What if it made her sick? What if it didn't work?

By the time Audrey, another of my patients, entered the treatment area, Annie had calmed her anxious thoughts enough to try to encourage the older patient.

'Welcome,' Annie said. 'Don't let that needle scare you. Debby's a pro at slipping it into your arm with almost no pain.'

For a moment, Audrey's tense expression morphed into a smile. Joy lifted Annie's spirits. At least she'd made someone feel a little better. She sipped a soda and then ran her tongue across her lips. Hey, she didn't have the usual bad taste in her mouth. Annie took a larger swig. She wasn't nauseous—not even a tinge.

Adjacent to Annie's chair, Debby adjusted the IV connected to Audrey. Annie caught her eye and gave her a thumbs-up. 'It's scary the first time around, but the fear is worse than the actual treatment.'

'Thank you,' Audrey said.

Annie smiled. By reassuring Audrey, she'd received far more than she'd given.

One week before Christmas, Annie returned for her second treatment. Although the clinic staff had decorated the office with festive accents, memories of last year's parties and late-night dancing clouded her spirit. She wondered if she'd ever return to that life. She was no longer the same person who walked through life unaware of the many blessings surrounding her. She'd never take her life for granted again.

Debby started the IV and the chemo.

'One step at a time, one day at a time,' Annie chanted as the new drug raced through her system.

After her third treatment in January, Annie returned to her surgeon. Tense with anticipation, she closed her eyes as he palpated the area surrounding her tumour.

'Annie?'

She opened her eyes to meet his intense gaze. Her heart slammed inside her chest.

'If I didn't know where it was, I might have missed it,' he said with a grin.

'Does that mean . . .'

He held up his hands. 'It means I want to send you for a CT scan to ensure the tumour has separated from your chest wall. If the CT confirms it, we'll schedule you for surgery and your tumour will be gone.'

Annie blinked at the moisture forming in her eyes. Cancer Act II had ended.

On the day of her surgery, Annie took a deep breath and stepped out from the car into the hospital parking lot. Instead of looking at the brick building, she gazed at the brilliant blue sky above. It was a glorious spring day. Overhead, the sun was slowly tempting the tiny green buds out from the trees lining the wide walkway. Birds chirped a merry tune as the scent of earth filled the air and new life wafted on the light breeze.

Beside her, Todd squeezed her hand as they continued in silence. In a few hours, Dr Jevel would have removed the last of her tumour. Once she recovered from surgery, she would move to radiation, and after radiation, she could once again look forward to life.

Dr Jevel completed Annie's surgery without complications, and after a short recovery, Annie came to see me. She wore a perpetual smile. For the first time since the diagnosis, the expression on her face reflected the gratitude filling her heart. She was going to live.

I opened the manila folder on my desk. 'So, Annie, how are you feeling?'

'Fantastic!'

I endorsed her reaction wholeheartedly. 'Dr Jevel called me after your surgery. He was very pleased with the results.'

Annie nodded. 'He thinks he got it all.'

I placed my hand on her shoulder. 'There's no evidence of the tumour. However, since the pathologist reported residual cells, I'd like to give you one more round of chemo after the radiation to make sure we've destroyed all the cancer cells.'

Annie didn't want to think about anything else at that point. The tumour was gone. She felt great. I paused to let her digest the information. 'Dr Jevel explained this, didn't he?'

'Yes. So the additional chemo is just to make sure we kill the last of the cancer cells, right?'

'I promised I'd always be honest with you. Your cancer has responded to the chemotherapy. I recommend you receive another round of chemo after the radiation therapy just to make sure we've killed any remaining cancer cells.'

'Okay,' Annie said, letting go of her elation just enough to revisit her motto 'One step at a time'. The next step was radiation.

On the first day of radiation therapy, Annie completed her usual morning hygiene with a persistent knot in her stomach. The curtain call for Act III in 'Annie's Cancer Saga' was scheduled at the radiation centre in less than forty minutes. Annie stiffened her spine. She'd endured chemotherapy and surgery. She'd make it through radiation. Besides, she had almost reclaimed control of her life and wasn't giving up on that goal now.

But the moment she entered the treatment room, her bravado sputtered. Okay, this was scary. With the chemotherapy, she had faced a silent battle inside her body. With radiation, she had to deal with an external force. Annie's eyes widened as she took in the huge machinery and the gurney beneath it. It seemed that her cancer saga had just entered the realm of sci-fi.

She turned to her imagination to help her through the first treatment. As the white robot-like machine emitted rays, she imagined she was back at work. In her mind, she was designing a new costume for a sci-fi flick. As the treatment progressed, she imagined various costume renditions. On most days, the treatment ended before she had finalized her design.

When Annie completed her last radiation treatment, the heat of August in South Carolina had parched the earth. As she emerged from the radiation centre, she didn't mind the sweltering heat.

It was over—chemo, surgery, radiation. Better, she was still walking in the sunshine—hot sunshine, but no way was she about to complain about the heat. She was alive. She had found a new job as a costume designer supervisor for Columbia Theatre. After a year of struggle with her health, she had not only re-entered the workforce but also secured a job in her chosen profession just sixty miles from her hometown.

One thing still hovered in the back of her mind—the last round of chemotherapy that I had recommended. By the time she returned for her next visit to my office, she'd made a decision. I entered the office with my usual smile. 'You've come a long way with a very difficult disease. I think with the radiation and one more course of chemotherapy, you have a good chance of keeping the cancer from returning.'

'I need a little more time,' Annie said.

I sat beside her. 'We'll continue to monitor you to help you live as long as possible.'

'No, I mean I'd like a little more time before I start another treatment.'

I was disappointed. 'I understand it's been a long process. But I think it's best to get one more course of chemotherapy just to make sure.'

'I plan to get the next course. I just want a little vacation. My uncle has an apartment in New York. When I was first starting in the theatre, I stayed there. I love the city. It has this exciting beat and it makes me feel so alive. I've put my life on hold during this treatment. I just want some time before I start up again.'

I closed her file. 'I understand your request. When you return, call the office and we'll schedule you.'

As Annie moved with the crowd from the subway to the street level, her heart strummed in her chest. She loved the city with its skyscrapers, busy streets and hustling workers. The minute she turned towards the theatre district on Seventh Avenue, her breath quickened. New York City wasn't always pretty, but it was always alive—especially near Times Square. The jitter of excitement danced through her veins and matched the beat of her flats on the pavement.

She'd just passed the mega toy store when a sharp pain speared through her lower back. Annie inhaled and moved closer to the building to let the throng of people shuffle past her. Maybe she had sprained her back lifting her luggage. With slow, measured steps, she made her way to the first restaurant, limped inside and eased into a seat near the entrance. In a few minutes, the pain subsided.

When the hostess asked to seat her, Annie shook her head and stood up. After a brief excuse about forgetting something, she turned towards the door. Okay, what was that all about? She continued to walk, but slowly.

The pain nagged her through the rest of the evening and into the night. When it continued the next morning, Annie thumbed through the Yellow Pages. According to some of her friends, chiropractors could fix simple backaches. After three calls, Annie made an appointment to visit a chiropractor only a few blocks from the apartment. Still walking like the Tin Man from *The Wizard of Oz*, she entered the office located on the second floor, over a butcher shop.

The staff greeted her with a smile and the chiropractor examined her in fifteen minutes. Annie received a spinal X-ray, a treatment to relax her back muscles, and instructions to ice the painful area until the strained muscles had time to heal. Relieved, Annie exited the office into the crisp autumn air. In eight to ten days she'd be as good as new.

Although Annie followed the chiropractor's advice, she experienced only temporary relief. But compared to cancer, a little pain in her back was a minor inconvenience. She finally had a life again. She planned to squeeze every moment of happiness and fulfilment from it.

In the third week of September, she returned home. The New York trip had revitalized her. There were so many things she was anxious to see and do, and returning to her cancer-patient status wasn't one of them. Yes, her back hurt a little, but she wasn't the only one on the planet plagued with backaches. Was it wrong to want a life free from blood tests, IVs and routine visits to the oncologist? After a night of soul searching, Annie called our office to speak with me.

'Annie, it's good to hear from you. How was your trip to the city?'

'Fabulous!' she said.

'Wonderful,' I replied. 'It's good to maintain a balance in your life. Are you ready for the final round of treatment?'

'That's what I called about. I feel great and I . . . I want a little more time to be Annie the artist, not Annie the cancer patient.'

'How much longer?' I asked.

'Just a few more weeks. I've got some things to do. I'll call for an appointment.'

By the last week of September, fall had moved into South Carolina. Although the sun still warmed the air to almost 80 degrees, the temperature in the evenings and mornings dipped. Annie loved the pastel hues of the evening sky as the sun slipped beyond the horizon. However, along with the drop in temperature came a more serious problem.

Tired from her hectic day, Annie had gone to bed early. Halfway through the night, she was jolted awake by a sharp pain in her abdomen. She rolled on to her side and tucked her knees into her chest, but the pain didn't ease. Within an hour, she rushed to the bathroom to empty her stomach.

With most flu bugs, once the stomach emptied, the pain subsided. But Annie received no relief. Worse, the vomiting continued.

'Honey?' Todd opened the door to the bathroom.

'Sorry I woke you,' Annie gasped between retches.

'Can I get you something? Water, Sprite, juice?'

Another round of vomiting made her stomach feel as if something was ripping it to shreds. She rested her forehead against the commode and gasped for breath.

'What time is it?'

Todd checked his wristwatch. 'Two-thirty.'

'You better get dressed. I think I need to go to the ER.'

The efficient ER staff drew blood and gave Annie an injection of Demerol, a potent pain reliever. From her gurney, Annie squinted at the wall clock. Todd's and her mother's voices droned in the background, but she couldn't focus on the words. Too bad the pain cutting through her abdomen didn't clear the haze in her mind.

'Have you ever had liver problems?'

From her near-foetal position, Annie blinked and tried to focus.

'Ms Carlson, your liver enzymes are high. Have you ever had liver problems?'

'No,' Annie said.

'When was your last chemotherapy?'

Why did he have to ask so many questions? Annie waited for the next wave of pain to pass. 'It's been a few months.'

'Alcohol consumption?'

'Stop the pain or go away!' Annie screamed in silence. 'I have an occasional glass of wine or mixed drink, but nothing lately.'

From the chair beside her, Todd said, 'Why? Is something wrong?'

'I'll have to perform more tests. It may be gallstones. I'll order an ultrasound and a CT scan. If we don't find something we need to treat on an emergency basis, we'll make an appointment for you to see your doctor for a follow-up.'

A week later, Annie, accompanied by her mother, came to my office. The pain and nausea had subsided, but her skin now had a yellowish tint, and she felt perpetually tired. Drained of energy, fear had returned to her mind.

I could not hide my concern. 'What has happened to you all of a sudden? You look quite low and depressed. You worry me.'

'Last week I had to go to the ER with a bad stomach pain. The ER doc said I had something wrong with my liver. He thought it might be from the chemotherapy until I told him it had been weeks since my last treatment.'

'What tests did they perform?'

Annie glanced at her mother, then back at me. 'CT scans. He told me to see you about the results.'

'Excuse me for a moment. I'll see if we have received them.'

Annie stared through the window at the garden. It was the first week of October and most of the plants had begun turning their leaves to red and brown. Was her cancer like those plants that would shed their leaves only to come back a few months later in full bloom?

The clock on the credenza softly ticked off the minutes. Fourteen minutes had passed since I had left to enquire about her CT results. Annie swallowed in spite of a cottony dry mouth. She knew I would never have kept her waiting needlessly. With each minute, her fear mounted.

Fifteen minutes later, I returned to the office with several sheets of paper. Despite efforts to remain reassuring, I'm sure I wore a crease of concern on my brow.

I placed the new sheets from the CT scan into her folder. 'Annie, I'm afraid your cancer has attacked your liver and bones. However, it's not the end of the world. We will continue to fight. We're not going to give up or cave in.'

Annie blinked. Had she heard me right? Was her cancer back—in two places? She counted her breaths—breathe in, breathe out. Her cancer was back. She knew the drill. Acquire information. Move on. She forced her eyes to meet mine.

'Please be honest with me—no sugar-coated language. You've been upfront with me so far, so please don't stop now. Is this it?'

I met her intense gaze, and she read the sadness in my heart.

'Do I have any treatment options?' she pressed.

'I promise I'll always be honest with you even if the news is hard for both of us. Annie, your cancer has come back with a vengeance. At this stage, we need to change our goals. Your cancer has spread to most of your bones and a large part of your liver. We have some treatment options. If we can't shrink the tumours, we may be able to keep them from growing.'

Beside her, Jill sobbed softly, but Annie kept her own tears at bay and breathed deeply to calm the waves of paralysing thoughts from clouding her judgement. Think. She had to think.

'Please, Annie. Don't give up,' I repeated. 'We can't just fold our hands and cave in.'

Annie pressed her fingers to her temples. This was so hard. She gazed at the ceiling and forced her thoughts into line. 'Okay, explain the type of treatments. How are they administered?'

Her questions eased the conversation a bit. 'There is a new compound called trastuzumab. It selectively targets breast cancer cells with the HER2/neu protein. We may add another drug to make it more effective and a bisphosphonate to help strengthen your bones and prevent fractures and pain.'

'Is that why I had the back pain while I was in New York?' Annie asked.

'That's a possibility,' I replied.

Her mother broke her silence. 'With this new treatment, are you talking about treating the tumour or just prolonging her life for a few months?'

'Every case is different, but there's a chance that the treatment will give Annie more time.'

Annie swallowed. The unstated part of my answer was clear. The cancer was back, and this time there was no talk of curing.

It would claim her life. She could go through more chemotherapy and gain more time. Around her, silence cloaked the room except for the clock ticking above my desk.

'I need time to think this through,' Annie said.

'Of course. You have my personal cell number. Call me if you have any questions.'

With her arm wrapped through her mother's, Annie left the clinic. She'd come full circle with her treatment. She wasn't cured. Her cancer had spread and it would soon end her life. How would she spend her remaining days—mourning her death or embracing each precious moment that remained?

After careful consideration, Annie agreed to the additional treatments. Every day was precious, and she wanted as many as possible. She decided to keep her morbid thoughts private. Her fate had devastated her family. Todd and her mum had been her cheerleaders, so hopeful. Why did her family have to suffer too?

That night, Annie fought the inevitable despair and sadness. However, with the sunrise, she resolved to live. She couldn't live forever, but forever had never been part of her life contract. She had now, this moment, and she planned to live it to its fullest. Small issues that had annoyed her in the past faded in importance. When she felt love and gratitude, she acknowledged it. She touched, hugged and talked with her loved ones. Since her moments were numbered, she planned to leave this world with a heart full of love, with no regrets or unspoken feelings.

Of course, there were low moments, but she did her best to keep them inside and only played the pity-party if she was alone and could do nothing to lift her spirits. During the day, Annie pasted a smile to her face and made it a point to make everyone around her feel life's joy. Although she was the youngest person in the infusion centre, she used her quick wit to entertain the patients and staff. She focused on laughter, not on nausea, and on the moment, not on tomorrow.

As fall faded into winter, Annie's jaundice deepened. In spite of her positive attitude, her bone pain increased until she had to limit her movements. I replaced her mild pain medications with instant-acting morphine. She would have to take a dose every six to eight hours to control her discomfort.

Although Annie was mostly able to live above self-pity, she had a hard time adjusting to the anguish her mother and Todd suffered. They, too, put on brave faces, but as her health deteriorated, she noted they were having more difficulty suppressing their emotions. One sunny morning, she woke up to find Todd weeping beside her. Similar incidents occurred during the day with her mother. Each time, the sight of their emotional torment hurt worse than the increasing bone pain that ravaged her body.

One evening, Annie swallowed her medication and pushed herself upright. 'I'm tired of lying around the house. It's almost Christmas. Let's go to the mall.'

Her mother's eyes widened. 'Honey, are you up to it? The mall will be a madhouse with shoppers.'

Annie took out her coat from the front closet. 'Sounds like just the thing I need—decorations, bustling people . . . Life,' she added silently.

Jill looked through the front window. 'It's very cold today. Maybe we should wait until tomorrow.'

'Mum, Todd won't be back for a few hours. Let's go shopping. If I get tired I'll sit in the common area, listen to Christmas music, and watch the people passing by.'

'You're sure?'

'I'm going. I'd like you to come with me.'

As Jill frowned, Annie suppressed a smile. It wasn't like she was trying to press her mother's buttons, but she needed to get out of the house. What better way than Christmas at the mall?

Just the act of getting in and out of the car and walking into the mall exhausted Annie. 'How discouraging,' she thought.

Then she stiffened her spine. Cancer had nearly claimed her body tissues, but that didn't mean she had to allow it to take over her mind and spirit.

'I love the Christmas decorations,' she said, using it as an excuse to stop and rest as she focused on a beautiful holiday wreath.

'Where do you want to go?' her mother asked.

'I want to sit on one of those sofas right in the middle of the action,' Annie said.

From her mother's frown, Annie guessed she was on to her ploy. However, it did not matter, because Jill entered a store to shop to distract herself from thoughts of her terminally ill daughter. And with that, Annie began to focus on the holiday season instead of her depressing disease.

'Do you have your cell phone?' Annie asked, as she sank into the plush cushions of the sofa. 'I'll call if I need you. Now go.'

'Do you . . .'

'You have my list. Now, go. I'm fine.'

As soon as Jill disappeared, Annie sighed in relief. Fatigue settled into every muscle as she focused on the busy shoppers. To her right, a child babbled excitedly about Santa Claus. Behind her, a young teen begged his parents for a loan to purchase a special gift. On her left, a lady struggled with so many bags that Annie wondered how she would get them to her car.

'Annie!'

She'd know that voice anywhere. Annie turned to her right as her mother's best friend and hairdresser approached with a large shopping bag.

'Jodie, it's good to see you!'

Annie caught the look of distress that Jodie quickly hid before she gave her a gentle hug. Did she look worse or was something else bothering Jodie?

'It's so wonderful to see you out. You're not alone, are you?'

'No. Mum had a few last-minute presents to buy, so I came along. I love this time of year.'

Jodie placed her shopping bag on the floor and sat on the sofa beside Annie. 'I love that pink sweater. The colour is perfect for you.'

Annie appreciated the compliment. The cancer had been brutal on her looks. However, something more important came to mind. 'I'm glad you're here.'

Jodie gave Annie's hand another squeeze. 'Me too, especially since you're here with me.'

'I have something important to talk to you about. It's big. Well, not really that big, but it could be . . . difficult.'

Jodie frowned. 'What's bothering you?'

'I need a favour.'

'You don't have to ask for a favour. Tell me what you need and I'll be happy to do it.'

Annie glanced at the crowd, then back to Jodie. 'Everyone thinks I'm going to beat this. But I think they're wrong. I think I'm running out of time.'

Jodie offered a weak smile of reassurance. 'You're just having a bad day and that's okay. But don't give up.'

'I want you to do my hair.'

Jodie checked her watch. 'I have an appointment in an hour, but I'll work you in.'

Annie resisted the urge to scream. This was so hard. 'After I'm dead.'

Jodie's eyes widened, and her mouth seemed frozen in the shape of a little 'o'.

'Don't look at me like that. Funeral homes hire people to style hair. I want you to do mine.'

With trembling fingers, Jodie lifted a thin strand from the side of Annie's face. 'Your hair was always beautiful. I remember the first time I cut it.'

'That's why I want you to do this. The chemotherapy has pretty much wrecked it, but you can fix it. I know you can.'

Jodie blinked back a tear. 'When the time comes, I'll do whatever you like. But right now you're alive. Every day scientists are discovering new drugs and treatments.'

'I'm not giving up. I just want to be prepared. You're a fabulous hairdresser and I want to look beautiful one last time.'

'You'll always be beautiful, Annie.'

'Like you have an unbiased opinion. Promise you'll work your magic on my hair. I want everyone to remember how I was before I got sick. I know my hair is not the same, but I've seen you work miracles. I need you to work one for me.'

Jodie swallowed, and then nodded.

'Thank you,' Annie whispered.

That request marked the beginning of Annie's preparations. If this was to be her last Christmas, she wanted it to be memorable for her family. Her treatments were the first to go. She called me and made two requests: Cancel all chemo appointments prior to Christmas, and write a prescription for a stronger, longer-acting pain medicine so she could enjoy her time with her family.

Annie resolved that her final Christmas gift to her family would be her spirit. She wanted to share the joy of laughter with her loved ones. When her back wrenched with pain, she laughed and made every effort to help others laugh with her. She focused on every witty remark in her repertoire and used them like she'd once used sequins on a costume—everywhere. She also made each day, each moment, sparkle with love and light. She had to cram those intense feelings of a lifetime into her remaining days. On the close of Christmas Day, as she kissed Todd and each member of her family, she whispered two quiet, simple words to each of them: 'Thank you.'

At Annie's request, I visited her home on 4 January. She greeted me with a smile and a 'Happy New Year!'

'Happy New Year to you too! How is your pain medicine working? Do you need another prescription?'

'How much time do I have?' she asked.

I hesitated. 'Excuse me, I wasn't prepared for your question.'

'Sorry, but I need to know.'

'I'm afraid maybe a few weeks or a month.'

Although she'd sensed her time was almost gone, this took a few moments for her to process. Then she asked, 'How will I die? Will it be painful, or will I slip into a coma?'

'I need to admit my ignorance here, because death may be different for each individual. But know that I won't let you suffer in pain. Whatever you need, you call me. If you can't, your mother or Todd can call. Day or night, I'll respond.'

Annie opened her palm, and I gently held it.

'Thank you. I needed to hear that first. I've had something new happen. I am not afraid of dying. I just don't want to suffer, and, more importantly, I don't want my family to see me suffer. I have . . .'

She paused. I waited for her to continue.

'I have a throbbing pain and a kind of electric sensation in my left arm and leg. What's that all about?'

'Those symptoms indicate the cancer may be invading your brain, if it has not already happened. If that is the case, you may slip into a coma before your death.'

Annie nodded. 'That's probably why my head hurts on and off.'

'Yes.'

'My family members are having trouble letting go.'

I cupped her hand. 'Where would you prefer to be when you die—at home or in a hospice?'

'I want to slip away from this world without difficulty. I think it will be very hard for Mum, Dad and Todd to witness me dying here.'

Annie blinked away sudden tears, then the corners of her mouth lifted into a smile. 'Thanks, Dr Patel. Your visit has been a tremendous help. I believe our relationship in this life ends here, and I have a lot to do to prepare. I look forward to seeing you. Maybe next time I'll be one of those hummingbirds outside your office!'

I couldn't speak. She gave me a weak hug, and I saw another tear making its way from the corner of her left eye. Goodbyes are never easy.

In the kitchen, Jill was preparing a light lunch. Lost in thought, she almost didn't notice my presence until I spoke.

'She's at peace with her disease,' I told her. 'I'm amazed at Annie's insight. She's in complete control and has accepted how she will move from this life to the next.'

Jill couldn't suppress her tears. 'I wish I could share her grace. It's so hard.'

I embraced her. 'If you need me, just call—at any time.'

The next day, Annie complained of severe headaches and nausea. She could barely move her left arm. Jill called 911 and rushed her daughter to the hospital. When they arrived, the ER physician contacted me. I requested a brain scan and left the clinic for the hospital. The medications they infused into Annie's system helped alleviate her pain and nausea, but she was confused and disoriented when I examined her.

As soon as the results from the scan arrived, I joined Jill, Trace and Annie's grandmother in Annie's hospital room. Todd had determined that he couldn't emotionally handle Annie's final moments, so he hadn't accompanied them.

'Annie's scan indicates multiple cancer spots throughout her brain,' I reported.

'How long?' Jill whispered in a strained voice.

'I don't think she'll be with us more than a few days.'

I folded Jill's hands into mine. 'If Annie slips into a coma and can't breathe on her own, do you want me to place her on a ventilator?'

'No! Doc, no! That's not going to happen to her. Please tell me that won't happen.'

'I don't believe she will go in that manner. However, the cancer has invaded her brain, and it could cause her brain tissues to swell at any moment. That swelling could affect her breathing. This is not the kind of decision you want to make quickly in the middle of the night. It's best if you make that decision now. If you like, I'll come back after you and Trace have had time to discuss your wishes.'

Jill and Trace exchanged glances. Trace lifted his shoulders in a resigned 'I don't know' expression.

Jill turned back to me. 'What do you suggest? What would you do if this were your child?'

'This is a terrible decision for a parent,' I acknowledged. 'Her cancer has behaved like wildfire until now. If you decide to place her on a ventilator, the chances are poor for her to ever come off it.'

'So we'd only be prolonging . . . this.'

After a moment I said, 'If my son had a similar prognosis, I wouldn't want him to be placed on a breathing machine.'

Jill looked at her husband and he nodded.

'No breathing machines and no CPR,' she said. 'We don't want to make her any more miserable. While I want to cling to my little child longer, I don't want her to suffer any more. Annie has accepted this. It's time for us to do the same.'

With tears streaming down her cheeks, she picked up her daughter's slender hand and gently rubbed it. On the other side of the bed, Annie's grandmother prayed for a peaceful departure. Trace lowered his head into his hands. I quietly left the room to make a note of the family's wishes. It would be the last action I would take in Annie's therapy.

Jill stayed at Annie's side. As she continued to caress the soft skin of Annie's hand, memories flowed through her mind. Annie had such beautiful hands. Jill loved the feel of them; she had loved washing her chubby fingers covered in cake and icing of her first birthday. She remembered praising her little girl as she washed traces of paint from her nails after her art class in second grade. She remembered crying when Annie held up her ring finger with Todd's engagement ring a few years ago.

Outside, the sun descended as Annie's breathing became irregular. Although she didn't open her eyes, her eyes moved beneath her eyelids as if she were dreaming. Jill watched, waited and remembered. Darkness filled the room. Annie's chest expanded and fell. A few moments passed before it repeated the movement.

Within a few hours, Annie was breathing barely two or three times each minute. Jill continued to gently rub her wrists, singing the nursery rhyme that Annie had sung as a little girl. Jill knew Annie was listening as she waited for her eternal sleep. Indeed, Annie was listening. A few moments before midnight, her eyelids opened. A tear, reflecting the moonlight, glistened in her eye. Jill's hopes rose for a moment, then she realized that Annie wasn't seeing. Annie took a deep breath, and her lids closed again.

Jill squeezed Annie's hand and waited. One minute . . . two minutes. Five minutes later, she slowly released her daughter's hand and placed it across her chest.

'Goodbye, Annie,' she whispered.

* * *

Harry had sat mesmerized as I recounted Annie's brave departure.

'Annie was the youngest patient to have passed away under my care,' I reflected.

'Oh my,' Harry said softly. 'What a life. She lived her dreams every minute. She did what she loved and spent time with whom she loved. Such a beautiful and calm farewell.'

Harry gazed out at the garden for a moment, then continued. 'I'm glad you were able to help Annie move on to her eternal flight with some peace and grace. Unfortunately, my mum's no longer alive to sing me my favourite lullaby when I'm ready to leave.'

He paused a moment, thinking. 'Susan is very tender at heart and I cannot see her accepting my departure without resistance. It will be hard on her, and on me too. But I will need to plan my departure well in advance.'

'I am not sure if that will be within your control, Harry.' I knew that he may not be aware of his surroundings during his final moments.

'Well, doc, didn't you say that Annie opened her eyes just before she flew out of this world? What makes you so sure that departing souls are not aware of what is happening around them?'

'You are right. I have not walked that path,' I said. 'Honestly, neither have I thought of it. I don't know how I'll take it when my own time comes.'

'Well, I don't want to hear any more of young people dying. Can you tell me about more mature people and how they handled their journey beyond this body?'

'Sure, next week, when we meet, we can talk about someone different. Maybe a teacher. I'm sure we both can learn from her. Her name is Julie. Sorry—her name was Julie.'

'Okay, doc. Thanks again for all your time. I don't know how you keep working with cancer patients on a daily basis, though. I'll see you next Wednesday.'

We rose from our chairs, and I could see tears in his eyes as he stood.

'Doc, I apologize for taking you back to what must have been very hard—not just for Annie, but also for you. I still have some questions that keep haunting me. What does it mean to die well? What do you think an ideal death looks like? How can I prepare Susan and my daughters to deal with my death?'

'Harry, one suggestion I'll make is that you start writing notes that enable you to share important thoughts with those you will leave behind. You can express your ideals, communicate lessons you have learnt from life, share memories and hopes, offer advice, ask for forgiveness and express love.'

He nodded, resonating with the idea. 'I'll start on that this week. And I want to start planning for my own funeral. If young Annie could do it, why not me?'

I walked him to the waiting room. I could see that moving about was getting more painful for him.

5

Death, You Lost Today

Death be not proud though some have called thee
Mighty and dreadful, though thou art not so;
For those whom thou think'st thou dost overthrow,
Die not, poor Death, nor yet canst thou kill me . . .
One short sleep past, we wake eternally,
And Death shall be no more; Death thou shalt die.

—John Donne

Harry's well-ironed khakis couldn't hide his weakening gait the following week, though his high spirits were evident from his shining face.

The last story had taken him for a turn. Thinking through the struggle that someone in their twenties, who hadn't even truly begun her life yet, had gone through and yet faced the fear and the sense of loss of the potential her life had, allowed him some emotional strength that alleviated his own burden. But though the strength of Annie's story guarded him emotionally, for the time being, it could do little to alleviate his worries.

He had to pause to take a breath as he walked outside to join me under the dome for our next session.

'So, doc,' he started the conversation, 'I heard you talked about me this morning in your board meeting. What did you guys think?'

'News travels faster than I thought,' I smiled back at him.

'Well, nowadays, Susan comes home for lunch.'

He paused, then explained, 'I did not know it would take stage 4 cancer to get her out of work to join me for lunch! Nevertheless, I count the blessings that I have. For my last few days of life, I can have her with me every day for lunch!' He sighed.

'It could have been worse, my friend,' I said. 'You could have been run over by a Mack Truck and then neither of you would have had the luxury of a daily lunch with your love. Nor would you be able to plan for your departure.'

'Doc, tell me about one thing. Last week you had said that, in spite of all your discussions, you cannot predict the time, mode, place or manner in which death arrives. If a person with your experience can't predict any of these, what does it mean to be alive? If death has the final word, how do we ordinary human beings live a happy, meaningful life? What does life mean?'

'Thinking about and meditating on my finality has shaken up my own lifelong awareness of the meaning and the purpose of living as a human being. How does one find meaning in the face of impending death? Living in daily awareness of death makes me tremble. Sometimes, I think, I would've been better in a plane crash. At least I would not be going through this turmoil.'

I had heard other patients voice similar thoughts. 'Harry, your reaction to our conversations is absolutely normal,' I said. 'Especially for people living in the US. The rest of the world has accepted the finitude of life and the finality of our time in the face of death. Outside of accidents, trauma, violence and guns, we have lost our awareness of death in the US.

'These questions about death have haunted humankind for years. Centuries ago, Greek philosopher Epicurus wrote that upon initial thought, it seems as if death is one of the worst things that can happen to us. However, upon more reflection and contemplation, it becomes more obvious that death cannot be considered bad for the person who is dead. Death, he proposed, is the privation of sense experience. Since we're not here to experience death, it can't be a bad experience for us. It isn't any kind of experience, so it can't be bad for us, in any sense.'

'Then how come the most worried person is the one who is dying? I'm not following.'

I continued, 'Epicurus suggested that the highest state of awareness is "ataraxia", or equanimity. It's a level of awareness that can cultivate a sense of freedom from the fear of death and its consequences. The elimination of intense mental and emotional ups and downs we experience results in this. Pleasure and pain are all one sensation for a person firmly established in equanimity. In the famous Hindu scripture Bhagavad Gita, Lord Krishna brings up equanimity to alleviate the fear of death and destruction from Arjun, his disciple, who is caught in a war between two royal families that almost ended life in ancient India.

'A great Roman philosopher, Lucretius, goes a step further. His argument was to imagine the infinite stretch of time that preceded our birth, pointing out that prior to our birth we were not bothered by non-existence through that vast period. Well, Lucretius argues, post-death non-existence is the same as pre-birth non-existence. Therefore, why do we need to worry? Since a person who is deceased lacks sense experience, why should he or she be bothered? While it is true that death deprives us of the goods of life, it is also true that the deceased will not be around to experience that deprivation.'

'I think I get it,' Harry said. 'I am slowly able to accept my own mortality. However, I need your help in preparing me to enable the transition of my family without me. As you know, Susan is very tender at heart and cannot let go of her attachment.

Her mother is in the memory care unit and has no other siblings or living relatives nearby who can enable her to deal with the grief of losing me. Her stepchildren all live in different parts of the world, at least twelve thousand miles apart. In fact, I think she pretty much has only you and your team to confide in emotionally and help her deal with bereavement.'

'Can you share a lesson from one of your patients who, like me, was more worried about their survivors than himself or herself? Last week you mentioned a teacher who was very much a giver. Tell me what happened to her after being diagnosed with advanced cancer and how she managed to prepare her family.'

* * *

I joined Julie's cancer journey on a beautiful, exhilarating spring day. I had planned to leave early because I wanted to spend time with my son, a high-school junior. Just as I headed towards my office door, my receptionist called.

'Dr Patel, I have a call for you from Dr Terry Hayes.'

Already tired from counselling two terminally ill patients for hospice care, I struggled to hide my displeasure with the interruption.

'He wants to speak to you as soon as possible,' she insisted. 'And only to you.'

'Put him through,' I said, as I lifted the receiver in my private office.

'Dr Patel? This is Terry Hayes. I'm a primary care doctor from York. I've heard great things about you and have a special request.'

'Yes?'

'One of my patients diagnosed two years ago with breast cancer suffered a stroke today. Could you see her?'

I tried to process the information. Prior to this conversation, I had never spoken to Dr Hayes. While flattered, I was also a little annoyed at my previously unknown popularity. I asked, 'Now?'

'Yes. She will need treatment as soon as possible.'

The real reason behind his generous praise surfaced in my mind. I was the only doctor in the office, and he wanted his patient seen right away. As I glanced at the garden tipped with new foliage outside my window, a moment of indecision filled me. Then, although I longed for the peace nature offered and knew that my son would be particularly unhappy that I was working late, I said, 'Please send her my way.'

Within thirty minutes, my assistant wheeled Julie into my office. Julie's husband, Joe, followed close behind. As soon as I saw the bewilderment and fear in Julie's eyes, I realized that her case would rob me of a much-needed night of sleep. Indeed, the details of her condition frightened me. A beautiful woman with a fair, flawless complexion, Julie appeared much younger than her stated fifty-five years of age. Dark brown hair framed her face, giving her a graceful appearance in spite of the partial facial paralysis.

As I started the examination, I asked, 'Can you tell me what happened?'

'We don't know,' Joe said. 'She was fine a few hours ago. Now she can't even stand or speak. Please help us.' Tears pooled in his eyes.

Julie, still in a state of shock, remained quiet. So I placed a hand on Joe's shoulder to help calm him. 'Let's start at the beginning. Tell me what happened.'

'Up until this morning, she was in perfect health. She had breast cancer two years ago, but they caught it at a very early stage.'

'Did she have surgery?' I asked as I continued examining her.

'Yes, and she takes a pill to keep it from spreading.'

The conversation seemed to help Joe regain control of his emotions.

I lifted Julie's right hand and asked her to squeeze my fingers. 'Tell me how the symptoms started.'

Joe tenderly touched her cheek. 'Julie teaches at the middle school. She was in the bedroom, getting ready for work. Right, honey?'

Julie nodded.

'She was brushing her hair when it started. At first, she couldn't lift her hand to finish her hair. Next, her right leg got weak. She couldn't stand up, so she slumped next to the dressing table.'

'Julie, can you lift your right leg now?' I asked as I pressed lightly against her lower leg. She managed a slight movement.

Joe continued, 'Thank God I was still at home. I heard her cry out and ran to the bedroom.'

More tears made tracks down his cheeks. 'I knew something was wrong the minute I saw her face. Then, when she tried to tell me what happened, I couldn't understand her. That's when I panicked and half dragged her to the car. I think I ran every red light on the way to the urgent care centre.'

Based on Julie's symptoms, I believed her tumour had invaded her brain tissue. As an oncologist, the diagnosis wasn't the most difficult part of my job. The hard part was explaining my suspicions to my new patient and her husband. I took a calming breath and faced them.

'Joe and Julie, I believe we are dealing with a serious situation here. Judging by the speed of her progressive weakness, I worry about what might come next. I want to admit her to the hospital right away.'

I paused to let them process the diagnosis. Then I warned, 'If her condition continues to worsen, we may need to place her on a ventilator to protect her airways.'

'Do you mean she's dying?' From the stunned look on Joe's face, I knew he and his wife had not considered life-support issues.

I tried to infuse my voice with reassurance. 'That's not what I meant. Not at all. We just need to be prepared. Her weakness could progress, making it hard for her to breathe. If that happens, she might need temporary breathing support until we figure out what's happening inside her brain.'

For this couple, the sudden transition from seemingly good health to terminal illness had made them desperate and vulnerable. I placed Julie's cool fingers between my palms. 'We will deal with whatever comes our way. I have had patients who have recovered from similar episodes. This is a serious situation, but don't lose hope. Patients with positive attitudes have the best success rate.'

Joe wiped tears from his cheeks. 'What do you think is going on in her brain?'

'I'll need to run tests to be sure. The weakness could be anything from a mild stroke to a full invasion of her brain by the cancerous cells.'

'Cancer. But she's been so healthy. We thought it was gone.'

'The chemotherapy may have destroyed the breast cancer cells, but sometimes those cells hide. After a while, they can reappear in the brain or other parts of the body.'

'Do you think the cancer has spread to other areas?'

'I don't know. While she's in hospital, I will order tests to give us this information.' I turned to look directly at Julie. 'I know this is very hard, Julie, but we need to talk about your wishes if the cancer has spread.'

Tears filled her eyes.

'Do you have a living will?' I asked.

Julie shook her head. From behind me, Joe said, 'No.'

'If the tumour has invaded a large section of your brain, you could slip into a coma. If that were to happen, do you want us to keep you on long-term life support?'

Julie's stunned gaze darted from mine to her husband's and back. She managed to shake her head.

Joe sniffed. 'She doesn't want to be filled with tubes and not know what's going on.'

'I'll write an order. The hospital staff will help you with the paperwork. Keep in mind that this is only a precaution for the unexpected. For now, let's focus on what's causing the problem. Once we know that, we can talk about treatment options.'

As the ambulance took over care for my new patient, I called the hospital to order a brain scan and blood tests to check liver and kidney function. I also contacted a neurologist to help me with her treatment.

The next morning, I stopped in front of the hospital room assigned to Julie. It was vacant. Momentary unease pounded at my chest. Had something happened to her?

I stopped a nurse in the hall. 'Where's my patient in room 555?'

She checked her schedule. 'Radiology.'

I relaxed. Nothing unforeseen had happened to Julie in my absence. However, that didn't alleviate my concern about what was happening inside her. Before long, I would know if there was a problem with Julie's heart or the vessels supplying oxygen to her brain.

The results of her brain scan awaited me at the nurse station. There was no brain tumour. However, the scan revealed that multiple small clots had clogged the circulation in her brain, causing minor repetitive strokes. I flipped the pages until I found the results of the blood work. Not good. Her liver function was grossly abnormal. I wrote additional orders in her chart and moved on to complete my hospital rounds.

Later in the day, I returned to Julie's room. She was propped up with pillows to support her weakened side. Joe sat in the vinyl-covered chair beside her. The sounds of a TV show filled the room. Joe turned down the volume when I entered the room.

I opened her chart. 'I've got some good news.'

Already encouraged by the decreasing paralysis, Julie and Joe turned to me. Hope brightened their faces.

'There's no evidence of a brain tumour.'

'Thank God,' Joe said.

I didn't want to exaggerate my good news, so I quickly added, 'However, the scan shows several small clots that have caused your symptoms. We have to figure out why they developed. You also have elevated liver enzymes, so I've ordered another scan of your liver.'

Still unable to verbalize her thoughts, Julie's head quickly turned from me to Joe and back. Joe nodded and asked, 'Do you suspect a liver tumour?'

'Julie may have small clots in her liver, just like the ones in her brain. If that's true, they could have caused the liver enzymes to elevate. We won't know for sure until after the liver scan. I've also ordered a test known as CA 27-29.'

Julie shrugged and raised her palms in question.

I pulled up a chair beside her bed to explain. 'CA 27-29 is a cancer protein that's released in the blood when a tumour is present. Women with breast cancer have elevated levels of CA 27-29. This test helps to tell us if your cancer has come back.'

When the colour left Julie's cheeks, I squeezed her hand. 'Try not to worry about the unknown, Julie. Right now, I want you to concentrate on healing. We have lots of new treatments available, but we won't talk about those unless necessary.'

When a stroke affects the communication centres, people often believe the patient can't express their emotions. This wasn't true with Julie. Although I had known her for only a couple of days, I had witnessed a myriad of emotions in her delicate features.

Her cancer journey had already proven to be a roller-coaster ride. I had seen her terrified by the onslaught of the stroke and the idea that her cancer may have returned, joyful when I had told her the scan had not shown a brain tumour, and now worried about the possibility of a liver tumour.

Like my patient, I, too, worried about what tomorrow would bring.

'I've left word with the staff to notify me the minute we have your results. When they contact me, I'll come to talk to you and Joe. In the meantime, try to keep a positive outlook.'

That evening, the paper in my hand described what had caused Julie's symptoms. But how would I present this information to them? Although I did my best to hide the despair I felt, I wondered if they would be able to read my emotions. The words to soften her test results simply didn't exist in the English language.

Joe pre-empted me. 'It's not good, is it, doctor?'

'No, I'm afraid it's not,' I replied as gently as I knew how to. 'The scan shows the breast cancer has invaded almost 8 per cent of her liver volume. Her cancer protein level, CA 27-29, is 6000. It should be 40. That means it's almost one hundred and fifty times the permissible upper limit.'

A tear trickled down Julie's cheek and she managed two words. 'What now?'

Her speech was somewhat garbled, but given the news I had just delivered, enunciation was the least of her worries.

'We need a liver biopsy to confirm that the tumour is malignant,' I said.

She struggled with her next question. 'Why me?'

Why? My mind went blank. Julie, Joe and I had celebrated the improvement of her paralysis and commiserated the threat of a terminal diagnosis. We were comfortable with one another, but how could I answer this question? Nothing in my medical training or previous patient cases had prepared me for 'why me?'.

Julie managed to speak. 'I am a Christian. Lived a good life. Faithful wife, teacher and mother.' She struggled to say this as tears welled up in her eyes and began trickling down.

I held her hand as she cried. After several minutes, her hand relaxed and the sobs stopped. 'How long?' she asked.

In spite of her broken speech, I knew exactly what she meant. End-of-life discussions are the most difficult part of my job, and no amount of training as a clinician or scientist can help. I had to present a real picture based on my knowledge of oncology. That picture was not pleasant.

'Each person is different, Julie. You could have a few weeks to several months. But please don't lose hope. I know patients with similar findings who have lived for years. Those cases are rare, but they have happened.'

Although I was apprehensive about Julie's future, she was transforming before my eyes from a passive, ill patient into a fighter. Her hands fisted on the mattress.

'Going to beat this!' she said.

'Of course you will,' I said, smiling, trying to infuse her with enthusiasm I didn't feel. Inside, my personal faith warred with my experience as a researcher, physician and oncologist. Science told me Julie could not possibly survive because her problem was not limited to liver cancer.

Since her original breast tumour had been less than a centimetre in size, her risk of developing systemic cancer had been less than 2–3 per cent. Yet she had developed liver cancer. The risk of stroke with her cancer pill, tamoxifen, was less than two per thousand, yet she had developed this rarest complication. It was as if she had already been selected for a perfect biological storm that could only end in death.

The litany of organic obstacles raced through my mind. She had failed standard treatments. She was battling her body's desperate attempt to confine the cancer to her liver by developing diffuse clotting and causing frequent strokes. She had also developed partial paralysis and still had difficulty speaking.

There was no way she could beat this. I knew the science and had experienced the outcome through other patients. I had been honest with her. Still, she was determined to fight and prevail.

Her intense gaze met mine. 'Will you help me?'

'Of course I will,' I said.

I started her on blood thinners to prevent the formation of more clots and reassessed her chemotherapy. Her current regimen had failed to prevent disease progression and might be contributing to her strokes.

Within days of her new regimen, Julie suffered another stroke and had to be hospitalized again. Again, her blood was clotting in a random fashion in spite of her present medication to prevent this complication. If I increased the blood thinner too much, I would increase Julie's risk of bleeding. It was risk management in every direction. After considerable research, I elected to start her on three different blood-thinner medications.

The day after admission, I stopped by her room during my morning rounds. Julie was in the bathroom and Joe was sitting in the lounge chair adjacent to her hospital bed. Although he greeted me, I could see the frustration in the tense set of his features and stiff posture.

'Tough day?' I asked.

'I don't know what to do. She's trying so hard, and nothing seems to be working. Maybe I should take her to Duke.'

'Duke is an excellent facility,' I acknowledged. 'If that's what you and Julie decide, I'll help you in every way I can.'

'It's not that we question your treatment. It's just . . .'

'I understand.'

The door to the bathroom opened, and Julie walked into the room. 'Hey, Dr Patel.'

Just as I turned to greet her, she crumpled to the floor. I quickly turned her on to her back and aligned her body, then felt for a pulse. Nothing. 'Run to the nurses' station and tell them to call a code,' I instructed Joe as I prepared to start CPR.

Within minutes the crash team surrounded Julie and she responded to our efforts. As soon as she was stabilized in the ICU, I took Joe to a private lounge to talk.

I placed my hand on his shoulder. 'She's stable and comfortable.'

Joe ran his hands through his hair. 'What happened?'

'Her blood pressure dropped too low and her heart stopped.'

Although I read the despair in his features, I couldn't tell him she was going to be all right because I knew the grim outlook. I outlined Julie's prescribed care for the next twenty-four hours.

Fortunately, Julie did not share our lack of optimism. Within a matter of days, she bounced back to her normal self. Her speech and muscle weakness improved and, within two weeks, I discharged her from the hospital. Given her determination and her amazing recovery, my hope returned.

One week after her discharge, Julie and Joe arrived at my office for her follow-up appointment. I had planned a candid conversation with them. Julie had experienced more complications than any of my previous patients. After her examination, I led Julie and Joe to my private office.

'Your case has been the exception to everything I've learnt in oncology medicine,' I began.

Julie merely smiled. Although her courage continued to amaze me, her determination moved me to continue the discussion. 'I've worked very hard to offer you the best care I know. Despite my best efforts, we haven't received positive results. I think it's time we go outside the area. You need a tertiary care centre that may offer you cutting-edge treatment.'

Julie's eyes held mine. 'I don't want to go anywhere unless you want to terminate my care as a patient.'

I raised my hands. 'It's not that I don't want to care for you. I only want the best for you.'

'I would rather die here than shift my care to another physician.'

I glanced at Joe. He shrugged. Julie's determination had not changed. She believed in herself, and she believed in me.

'Okay,' I said. 'You realize we're swimming upstream with your care, but we're going to treat your disease with everything we have in our arsenal.'

Julie nodded. 'I'm glad we understand each other. Tell me what I need to do.'

I adopted a very aggressive treatment plan and Julie met me toe-to-toe. We resumed chemotherapy, and she took daily blood-thinner shots. Over the next three months, her turnaround was just short of miraculous. She didn't just improve; she made a major comeback. Her next cancer assessment indicated her tumour-protein level had reduced to almost half of the starting point. Our once-thin ray of hope was quickly expanding.

Months of chemotherapy followed, along with the progressive shrinking of tumour size and activity. Finally, her cancer assessment resulted in a protein level within normal limits. To top off the blood analysis, her scans didn't show any tumours in her entire body. Within six months, after several near-death encounters, Julie had achieved complete remission.

We celebrated her physical improvement, but more amazing was her mental and spiritual improvement. Julie embraced life. She savoured her blessings and took note of every gift life offered. Of all my patients, Julie's case had topped the list in complication and severity, but the highs overrode the lows. As I reviewed her treatment plan, I realized that Julie had managed her cancer journey far differently from many of my other patients.

She hadn't permitted her physical suffering and pain to intimidate her. Instead, she had used the challenges to improve her strength. The cancer had given her the ability to think about life beyond the physical body. She had focused on her eternal and unending relationship with God, and with her daughter Laura, son Clint and husband Joe. She prayed to become a conduit for God's will. With her new perspective, she no longer viewed her existence only as a physical embodiment. She saw this life as part of an eternal life.

With no further evidence of a tumour, I stopped her chemotherapy. The disease no longer interfered with her life. Although Joe didn't overcome his fear of the cancer's return, Julie moved beyond the fear and lived in the present. Her cancer was in remission, and she focused on her life, not her death.

On the first anniversary of her initial diagnosis, Julie's life had returned to normal. Her scan revealed no viable cancer spots. Her blood work showed no cancer proteins, and we expanded the time between her check-ups.

The following spring, Julie and Joe planned a romantic getaway to Myrtle Beach—their first vacation since her stroke. They had booked a hotel for a week and were anxious to spend quality time alone.

Joe called the evening before their scheduled departure. 'Dr Patel, Julie is very sick. She got a headache and thought it was just a sinus infection. But Tylenol didn't help and now she's throwing up and tossing in bed from the pain. We were supposed to go to the beach tomorrow, but she can't travel like this. I don't think she can even make it to your office.'

I could tell by his urgent tone that Joe was in a state of panic. 'Take her to the ER. I'll try to be there when you arrive, but in case you beat me there, I'll call ahead and let the ER doctor know what to do.'

'I don't know if I can get her to the car.'

'Call an ambulance. I'll leave now and meet you there.'

On the way to the hospital, I phoned the ER doctor and ordered intravenous steroids and a CT of the brain, stat. By the time I arrived at the hospital, Julie had been admitted, and she was terrified. Her speech was incomprehensible, she had left-side paralysis, her body was stiff, and she was vomiting and writhing in pain.

I reviewed her test results with dread. Her blood tests had failed to reveal tumour recurrence, but the scan indicated multiple small tumours in her brain that had caused her brain to swell. She also had three large tumours at the back of her head.

I brought Joe and their daughter, Laura, into Julie's room. The medication to relieve her pain and reduce the swelling had started to take effect. Julie was drowsy but aware of her surroundings.

'Is it cancer?' Laura asked.

I nodded. 'Unfortunately, it's back. Julie's tumour has invaded her brain and caused swelling. The medication I've ordered will help relieve that swelling along with her pain and nausea. Can you tell me how long she's had the headaches?'

'On and off for the last few days,' Joe said. 'I didn't think that much about it because she's been in remission.'

'You didn't know,' I reassured him.

Joe ran his hands along his thighs. 'How did it come back?'

'Cancer cells can be tricky. Sometimes they come back in the brain or the spinal cord. The brain acts as a sanctuary for breast cancer. Before we had effective chemotherapy, patients didn't live long enough to experience brain metastases. Now, we know they hide in the thin layer that covers the brain.'

'She should have stayed on the chemo,' Laura said.

'I don't believe continued chemotherapy would have prevented this.'

'What if we'd done more scans?' Joe asked.

'Recent studies have shown that regular scans don't change the outcome.'

Although I tried my best, my explanation of the science didn't reduce Joe's sense of guilt. I was unsure if he had difficulty understanding the scientific concepts or if he just couldn't accept that advanced fourth-stage cancer often recurred regardless of best efforts.

'So I didn't do anything to hurt her chances?' he asked.

'No, Joe. I'm sure your love and support helped her remain in remission for this long.'

Laura asked, 'How can we help her now?'

'We've started IV steroids to reduce the swelling in her brain. Her situation is close to the way it was the first time I treated her.' I gave them a few moments to digest this information, then continued. 'I don't want to minimize her situation, but don't forget how she surprised us the first time around. Julie's a fighter and a survivor. She can do it again.'

I turned to Julie, who had opened her eyes and was watching me. 'This is not the end,' I said to her and her family. 'We still have effective and viable options available. Don't give up.'

As Julie replied with a weak smile, my resolve strengthened. We were going to fight back and prevail again, although for a finite time.

I admitted Julie to the oncology floor and called a neurosurgeon and a radiation oncologist to consult on her treatment. The neurosurgeon responded the same day. After an expanded exam, he recommended surgery. In the meantime, the steroids had started to reduce the swelling and pressure on her brain. Julie noticed a significant improvement in the ability to move her left arm and leg. Her seizures stopped along with her headaches. More importantly, her speech improved so she could communicate. During this phase of her disease, her resolve didn't waver. More amazingly, she continued to provide courage and support to her husband and children.

In a delicate operation, the surgeon removed three large, superficial brain tumours. But due to their depth and invasion into the brain tissue, he could not remove the multiple small tumours scattered throughout her brain on both sides of her head. We started whole-brain radiation to attack the small tumours and placed Julie on oral chemotherapy to enhance the impact of the radiation on the cancer.

Julie continued to improve. Within forty-eight hours, her surgical dressing was removed, and she was almost back to her normal functional level. I discharged her within the week. Within three weeks, she resumed her normal daily activities.

For the following month, Julie received daily radiation. She continued her medication for another three months and then wanted to know if her tumours had stopped growing. I ordered a brain scan. Whenever I receive scan results, I feel a wave of adrenaline prior to reading them. Will it be good news, or will I be telling someone that his or her time on earth is coming to an end?

I had already witnessed Julie's determination, but the scan results surprised me. As I read through the radiologist's interpretation, I viewed the film copy and blinked in amazement. Most of the tumours had stopped growing and two had shrunk to less than half their original size.

Life had changed once again for Julie. For now, our aggressive treatment had suppressed growth. However, Julie's long-term prognosis was not as encouraging. Our experience and research indicated a high probability that the cancer would return in the near or distant future. When I relayed an honest assessment to Julie, she seemed undaunted. We had suppressed her tumour growth, but the cancer had not suppressed her determination to explore options for another remission.

On a beautiful day in September, Laura accompanied Julie to my office for a follow-up visit. After I finished my exam, Julie said, 'Is . . . there anything else for my brain? I want to see my grandchildren grow.'

'Other than radiation and the temozolomide we've used, I don't know of a treatment to eliminate tumours inside the brain. Gamma knife or stereotactic brain surgery has been successful, but you have too many spots to treat on an individual-tumour basis.'

'How about going to some other place? Are the resources here good enough?' Laura asked as Julie nodded.

From the quick glances between mother and daughter, I guessed they were uncomfortable about suggesting another facility and physician. But second opinions are common in oncology, and I encourage my patients to explore all options. To me, the most important component of successful treatment is a patient's attitude towards care. If another opinion can make my patient more comfortable with the treatment plan, the odds may improve for a better outcome.

'I would love to explore all the possibilities for you. I can contact Duke University Medical Center. They have a distinguished reputation as a brain cancer centre. However, if you have another place in mind, I'll be happy to contact them for you.'

Laura's stiff shoulders relaxed. 'Spartanburg is closer to home, and we learnt they are connected to the MD Anderson Cancer Center. Would you mind if we see Dr East?'

I froze the smile on my face to hide my disappointment. Laura and Julie had not chosen a tertiary centre and a physician with more experience. Their choice would only be a lateral move. After what we had experienced together, I had thought they were satisfied with my skills and treatment.

'Hold on a moment,' I said as I busied myself with Julie's file and papers.

As I pretended to search for numbers, I tried to view the situation from Julie's and Laura's perspective. Julie and her family continued to shoulder a tremendous burden of fear and uncertainty. Their request to change care could be physician fatigue, a common problem that develops from long-term bouts with a terminal illness. Besides, they were looking for a ray of hope and continued reassurance, and it was my job to help them in any way I could.

'I'll make arrangements to transfer your care to Dr East. However, I will be more at ease if you also consult an expert in the field.'

Although they seemed to agree, I didn't think they were going to take my advice.

A week later, Dr East called to discuss Julie's case. I explained my treatment plan and rationale. Although it was a cordial conversation between physicians, Julie's new oncologist and I disagreed on one treatment option. I was afraid to start Julie on an anti-oestrogen pill because of her history of multiple strokes. I suggested systemic intravenous chemotherapy based on her positive response in the past. He felt the anti-oestrogen pill was worth the risk and Julie could avoid the side effects of the systemic chemotherapy. Since Julie suffered neuropathy, with lack of sensation in her hands and feet and the spontaneous sensation of burning pain, I wondered about their final decision.

I was unaware of the treatment choice Julie and her new oncologist made. Although the question haunted me, I didn't feel it was my place to enquire further. Julie had made her choice, and I needed to honour it. Besides, I had other obligations. In addition to my own practice, I was struggling to coordinate terminal cancer care for my mother-in-law ten thousand miles away in India.

I had just returned from a gruelling trip there. In addition to the length of travel and the time change, I had also said my final goodbyes to my mother-in-law, because her disease had progressed to the end stages and I wouldn't be able to make another trip soon. Due to my absence, I had a large patient load to catch up on and I still suffered from jet lag and the impending loss of a beloved family member.

During one of the few moments I had for a break, my receptionist called. 'Dr Patel, Julie is on the phone. Can you speak to her?'

My fatigue evaporated. 'Yes, transfer her call.'

'Hey, Dr Patel. This is Julie. Do you remember me?'

'Of course, Julie! I never forget my patients, no matter where they are.'

Silence filled the line, then Julie said, 'I've been hurting in my hands and feet, and I couldn't get an appointment to see my doctor soon enough. Is it okay if I come and see you, even though I've moved to another doctor?'

Two feelings rushed through me—delight that Julie wanted me to see her, and curiosity about her progress. I also felt a little hesitant. I didn't want her to feel she had to see me because her physician's schedule was full.

'Whenever you wish to see me, I will see you. However, if you prefer, I can call your physician and ask him to see you right away.'

'That's not necessary. I just want to see you,' she replied, without a moment's hesitation.

'Do you want to come today or tomorrow?'

'Laura's not home today. Can I come tomorrow?'

'Just tell my appointment desk when you'll be coming. Tell them to fit you in even if my schedule is full.'

'Thank you,' Julie said, relief in her voice.

The following day, Julie and Laura arrived at the office. As I greeted them, Julie's eyes avoided mine as she settled into the chair near the examining table. 'How's your mother-in-law?' she asked.

I shook my head. 'I think I said my final goodbye on my last visit.'

'I'm sorry to hear that.'

I sensed she had something she needed to discuss, so I waited as she studied her hands before looking up to meet my gaze. I smiled to encourage her.

'Dr Patel, I apologize for moving to another doctor. It wasn't that I was dissatisfied with your care. We just had to be sure there wasn't something else we could do. I like Dr East, but even after three months . . . it just isn't the same. I couldn't talk to him like . . . it's not the treatment. Actually, I am doing well, at least as good as can be expected. It's just—I just wanted to see you, face to face, so I could ask you to take over my care.'

A tear formed in the corner of her eye and everything inside of me seemed to melt. I hugged her as she wept.

'I'm so sorry,' she said.

'You don't need to apologize. I understand.'

After a moment, I released her and offered a box of tissues. She extracted one and wiped her face. 'You understand?'

'I would have done the same thing. When faced with cancer, you often need a second opinion. Treating patients is not about building my ego. I prefer that my patients seek a second opinion. My intelligence has a limit and I follow the treatment path I have learnt. There is always someone out there who may have more knowledge.'

'It's okay, Mum,' Laura encouraged.

'Let's talk about you,' I said. 'Do you have any health concerns?'

Julie shook her head. 'Just the tingling and numbness in my hands and feet. Once in a while, I have occasional burning sensations. Besides those, I don't have any other issues.'

'What about medication?'

'I'm taking letrozole. Do you want me to continue it?'

'Let's not rock the boat while the wind's in our sails. I want to see you in six weeks. I'll continue checking your blood work for cancer and, if needed, we'll order more scans.'

The tight set of Julie's features upon her arrival had relaxed and she now met my gaze with a bright, engaging smile. Her smile had supported me during the difficult times of her treatment and now I realized how much I had missed it.

Four weeks later, I opened an email from Julie. Dread picked at the edges of my mind as I read the words 'new headache'.

'Come to my office tomorrow,' I typed.

As a physician, I know the probable disease course for each of my patients. That knowledge does not make the process any easier. From the moment I received the email until Julie arrived the following afternoon, my mind had filtered through the possible sources of her problem. As soon as my office technician had recorded Julie's vitals, I started my examination of her muscle tone.

'How long have you had this headache?'

'Just a couple of days. This time around, I didn't blow it off as a sinus condition.'

I asked her to squeeze my hands with hers. 'Any other new symptoms?'

'No.'

Her right foot responded to the tickling sensation I stimulated.

My inner tension eased. The exam didn't indicate signs of a new tumour. 'Everything looks good today, but I want you to go for an MRI to ensure there's no new tumour in your brain.'

As she prepared to go home, I wrote a prescription for the headache. 'Make an appointment in one week, and we'll go over the MRI results and make further plans. Call me if the pain doesn't go away, or you have new symptoms.'

The following week, I prepared for my conversation with Julie. Although the physical exam had been negative, the MRI was far from it. As usual, she arrived on time for her appointment and made herself comfortable in my private office. Again, Julie displayed a calm grace that never ceased to amaze me. Like me, she knew the possible outcomes of the MRI. Did she feel as calm as her outward appearance suggested?

'The MRI shows your tumours are trying to get out of hand again,' I said.

Julie's expression didn't change.

'The tumours are swelling, and that's causing your headaches. Do you have any other symptoms?'

Julie shook her head.

'Good. I don't think we need to worry about brain herniation, but I want to resume steroids to reduce the swelling. There's a new drug approved for breast cancer that's moved to the brain. It's given with a small molecule called lapatinib. I want to start you on the two drugs.'

'Okay,' Julie said.

I wrote the prescription. 'This combination can affect your blood count, so you'll need to come and see me weekly.'

'What are the side effects?'

'The most common side effect is something called hand-foot syndrome.'

She stared at the prescription I had handed her. 'Is it like the burning I've had before?'

'A little. This syndrome involves on-and-off swelling, redness and pain in your hands and feet. You may also see skin peel off. Some patients experience diarrhoea and an upset stomach.'

Although she didn't say anything, I could sense she was weighing the pros and cons of the new drugs.

'I'd like to keep a close eye on side effects, so let me know if you have one of those symptoms or if anything new happens,' I continued.

She stood to leave. 'Okay, and thanks for watching out for me. It's nice to have a doctor who is available. There are so many changes.'

'You know you can call or email me any time.'

I waited, sensing there was something else on her mind.

After a brief pause, Julie said, 'One more question. How long do you think I have left?'

Julie had maintained such a positive approach to life and death that her question caught me off guard. I took a moment to frame my answer. 'I don't know. You've beaten the statistics more than once. If I were to follow strict science, you have survived three years beyond my initial expectations. Your strength and determination have made me look at cancer and survival from a new perspective. However, I don't play God. If I see signs for concern, I will let you know.'

'I'll see you next week,' she said with a nod.

I had been honest, but only God and Julie's body knew when death would arrive. The answer rested inside of Julie, not in me.

As spring ushered in a palate of yellow daffodils, pink cherry blossoms and white pear blossoms in our healing garden, Julie began her new treatment. Like the renewed life of nature, Julie made efforts to renew her own life. She increased her time outdoors with her two dogs. When she tired of tossing a stick or their favourite toy, she curled into a garden chair with philosophy books on life and death. Her headaches had subsided with the new treatment, and she didn't experience much of the side effects. After three months of chemotherapy, she returned to my office for the results of a follow-up body and brain scan.

The warmth and sunshine had given a light glow to her complexion, helping mask her cancer. She greeted me with a smile, and I escorted her to my office.

'Julie, we have good news and bad news,' I said, opening her file. 'The good news is the tumours in your brain have stopped growing. Our new chemo combination seems to have been effective.'

Although she smiled, her face told me she was bracing for the bad news.

'The bad news is that your body scan shows something in your back, about neck level.'

I approached her and touched the area from the base of her skull to her shoulders.

She rotated her neck. 'I don't hurt there. I can move my head fine.'

'Maybe we've caught it early. The radiologist recommends we get a CT scan or MRI of your neck vertebrae to see what's there.'

'Why? If you find something, can you cure it?'

I blinked in surprise. When she said she didn't hurt, she was trying to tell me she didn't want to hear or deal with anything else. I had been so intent on finding and treating the disease that I had missed her code. 'It depends on what we find there. If it's a tumour, we can control it for some time. If it's something else, maybe we can help you there too.'

Julie hesitated. Then she said, 'I'll do it only if you can cure it. Otherwise, leave it there and see if it starts bothering me. If it becomes a problem, we'll deal with it then.'

Although it was her decision, I presented a rationale to change her mind. But she was resolute. 'There may be more microscopic tumour cells floating around everywhere. I don't want to chase every one of them. Besides, I've just completed my third anniversary of my new cancer and I'm still here. Isn't that great? I'm ready for anything now.'

My argument for additional treatment died. Julie was listening to her body. Perhaps she was also listening to her Maker. She had accepted that her time was running out. For Julie, the only remaining questions were when, where and how. And the answers to those questions had nothing to do with me or medicine.

I felt a wave of sadness when Julie left the office, and I still had other patients to see. I knew I wouldn't be able to give my patients the care and attention they deserved, so I asked my partner to fill in for me. On the drive home, I replayed my encounter with Julie. She wasn't arrogant or abusive, only assertive. She was in control of her final days and wanted to remain that way.

I checked my motives. Control had never been something I needed or craved, but I didn't want to let Julie go. She had brought strength and determination to my life just as she had brought them to her family. She was one of those rare individuals who enriched and enlightened everyone she touched. Was it wrong to want to preserve the gift she brought to all of us for as long as possible?

Three weeks later, my cell phone jingled. Caller ID showed it was Julie.

'Dr Patel, I hate to bother you first thing on a Monday morning, but I have pain in my hands and feet. I feel bloated and weak, and it feels like a band is tied around my neck and upper arms.'

There was deep concern in her voice.

'Is someone with you?' I asked.

'I also had trouble passing urine a little while ago. I don't know what's happening. I feel weak everywhere.'

I gripped the phone. 'Julie, are you alone?'

'Joe hasn't left for work yet.'

I relaxed my grip. 'Go to the ER and call me as soon as you arrive.'

As I prepared to meet Julie, anxiety washed through me. If my preliminary diagnosis was accurate, Julie had developed spinal cord compression—an oncologist's worst nightmare. As tumours grow, they can put pressure on the spinal cord. In most patients I had seen who suffered spinal cord compression, the pressure resulted in complete paralysis and death from respiratory centre failure. I called the ER doctor, apprised him of my suspicions, and gave him instructions to follow if my diagnosis was correct.

As soon as Julie reached the hospital, the ER physician verified her symptoms and ordered an MRI of her neck and thoracic vertebrae. The results confirmed my diagnosis—the tumour was growing from within the spinal cord's central canal. In tumours arising outside the spinal cord, surgery can salvage some of the functions. However, intramedullary tumours such as Julie's represented a death sentence coupled with great suffering.

An hour later, the treatment team consisting of the radiation oncologist, the neurosurgeon and me convened and agreed on appropriate action. I started steroids to relieve pressure. We initiated radiation the following day. The neurosurgeon only recommended comfort care because he felt the tumour was too invasive for surgical removal. The rest was up to Julie and God.

Within a few days, the steroids had reduced the swelling around the spinal cord and Julie could stand and walk with help. Her bowel and bladder symptoms had also improved. On the fourth day of her hospitalization, I entered her room to discuss her wishes for the future.

Inside the single-patient room, Julie was settled in a large easy chair near the bed. I pulled up the small guest chair. At first, I thought she might be sleeping, but then her gaze lifted from her hands, and she offered her usual smile. However, her eyes and the slow release of air before she spoke hinted of resignation.

'I was just thinking of you,' she said.

'I need to know your wishes on how to proceed.'

She gave me a sad smile and said, 'I've had my share of ups and downs, and I've enjoyed every moment of my life. I've taken all that God has granted me with gratitude. You've done your best to help me through these difficult times and I appreciate your efforts.'

A tear trickled down her cheek, and I took her small hands in mine. This was Julie's time to talk. I waited for her to continue.

'I don't know how you can do this over and over again. You make it easy on people like me.'

'I do this because I believe it's my mission. Helping people like you is the reason I chose this life.'

Her chin trembled as she forced another smile. 'I know I'm not going to live much longer. If reincarnation is true, I would like to be reborn and work with you. Maybe we can share some of the agonies you experience.'

'Let's talk about me another time. It's time to get you out of the hospital. You need to be home with Joe and your kids and your dogs and grandkids.'

She nodded her approval and opened her arms for an embrace. 'Thank you,' she whispered.

I wrote the orders on her chart and stood to leave. 'Don't forget to make an appointment to see your radiation doctor and me.'

She merely smiled. As I walked down the busy hospital corridor, I wondered what her lack of response meant. Did she want to see me again? Had her thank you really meant goodbye? She had limited time left with her family. And only she had the right to direct how that time would be spent.

When she missed her radiation appointment, the physician notified me. I wasn't surprised. Julie hadn't called for an appointment with me either. I considered calling her but held off. The decisions facing Julie were difficult, and she would need space to consider her options.

As if tuned in to my thoughts, Julie called the next morning. 'I don't want to offend you, but I've decided to stop treatment,' she announced.

'I understand' was all I could think of to say.

'I would like you to give me a home hospice referral,' she added, rushing her words together.

Why was she in such a hurry? Was someone waiting for her? The answer swept through me as I realized that this might be our last conversation.

I fought the tightness in my throat. 'Of course, I'll call them right now. Do you want me to continue to be your doctor for the hospice care?'

'Yes. I want you to be with me through the end. We started this journey three years ago. You can't abandon me before my departure.'

Emotion welled up inside me, and I struggled to control my voice. 'May I ask for a special favour? May I stop by your house to see you?'

She didn't hesitate. 'My door is always open for you.'

A tear made its way down my cheek. 'Will you check with Joe and your children? I don't want to take away from your private time with them.'

I waited as she covered the receiver and spoke with her family. 'No problem. Come at your convenience.'

'I'll visit you this evening.'

Julie lived in a small rural town located about an hour's drive from my office. As I passed the small homes and farms, memories of her filled my mind. Julie had faced cancer with determination and strength. I had witnessed those attributes in other patients, but Julie was different, because, with each severe test the disease imposed, she only rose higher.

Now she had chosen to close out her journey, and I wanted to offer whatever support I could. She had faced so much. I prayed she would be able to face death with the same dignity with which she had faced life. I checked my written directions and then turned into a modest neighbourhood and identified her house by the long yard and the large dog house. I gathered my emotions as I parked and approached the house. Although the front door was open, I rang the bell.

'Come on in, Dr Patel! I'm all the way inside.'

Julie was waiting in her wheelchair in the living room. To her right, a pet gate divided the living room from the adjacent room. Behind the barrier, two large chocolate Labrador retrievers watched us with liquid brown eyes.

I hid my sadness as I smiled and greeted her. No wonder her canine companions constantly watched over her. They didn't need to evaluate her weight loss and her drawn, weak appearance to know she was approaching the end of her journey.

She motioned for me to sit in a comfortable armchair. 'Times have certainly changed. The last time a doctor visited my house was almost forty years ago. I didn't know they made home visits any more.'

My mind groped for an adequate answer. I frequently made home visits, but that wasn't why I was here. How did I tell her I wanted to see her—that I needed to say goodbye?

'I still make home visits. It keeps me grounded and allows me to get to know the people who have trusted me with their lives.'

'I'm glad you came. I've been thinking about our journey together.'

I nodded.

'Remember the last time we talked in the hospital? There was so much I wanted to say to you, but I couldn't put my thoughts into words after the stroke. That's probably the most frustrating part of the process. Time is so precious and yet you can't verbalize your thoughts and feelings. Facing death is one thing. Facing death without being able to talk to your loved ones . . . well, that's terrible.'

I waited. Her speech had improved, but she still needed additional time to form her thoughts. Her smile was full of compassion. 'I just wanted to tell you how thankful we are for the time you gave us. We're going to miss you.'

She touched her cheek with a tissue to stop a trail of tears. 'Life's journey is truly unfathomable. Four short years ago, Laura married and joined the business with her dad. I thought it was time for Joe and me to slow down and enjoy life together. Then my cancer came back and everything changed.'

Her gaze took on a faraway look as she slowly shook her head. 'Three per cent chance of recurrence and I was in that 3 per cent. Now I know why.'

Her words brought my thoughts to a halt. One of the dogs whined and moved closer to the gate. His broad muzzle poked between the floor and the bottom of the barrier separating him from Julie.

'It's okay,' she reassured him before turning back to me. 'God enabled me to live my life to the fullest—fuller than most others get to live. He placed me on notice so I could experience His blessings every day. I thank Him for giving me cancer so I could experience His creation and enjoy His glory in every aspect in the limited time I had left on earth.'

I blinked in amazement. Julie was thankful for what she had experienced.

Unaware of my internal reaction, she continued, 'You brought happiness to me, Joe and my family by adding three meaningful years to my life. I'm ready. God has been giving me signals every day. My legs stopped working yesterday. I now have difficulty lifting my hands. He's giving me hints that He's ready for me. It's just . . .'

I placed my hand on her shoulder as her thin shoulders trembled with emotion. After a few moments, she regained control. 'I don't want to give up. I can't tell you how hard it was to cancel my appointment with you. I didn't want to hurt you, but I needed to start preparing for my journey. I prayed for help. He guided me to call you so we could talk. And I'm sure He inspired you to come here today.'

'You're not giving up. You're moving forward,' I said, trying to affirm her.

She pointed to a photograph of her wedding day with Joe. 'We were so happy that day. How can I leave him behind?'

She pointed to another photo. 'Those are my grandkids in the small silver frame. Don't you look forward to watching your grandkids grow?'

'Very much,' I said.

'Look at these sweet dogs . . .' She sobbed again.

'Goodbyes are the most difficult part,' I offered. 'But we can be thankful we are given a chance to say them.'

Although the tears continued, she seemed more at peace as she said, 'That's why I wanted to see you. I'm sure you've had to say several farewells. I still don't understand how you continue to do this without burning out.'

'This is the reason God put me here. I learn so much from my patients.'

'Maybe we've learnt together. The first time I came to your office I was a hopeless mess. I thought I had lost control, but you made me realize that wasn't true. You showed me I was in control. Your visit has reminded me I'm still in control of when I make my final departure—with the Lord's blessing. I needed this moment of decision-making power.'

I hugged her close, listening to her breathing. Once she quieted, I said, 'I truly believe God is ready for you. He inspired me to make this home visit today. Neither of us would have been able to put closure to our journey together.'

I released her and took her frail hands in mine. 'We were destined to meet in this life. And we'll meet again in heaven.'

We sat quietly together. Soon, it was time for me to leave. Although saddened by my impending loss, I was grateful for the opportunity to speak what was in my heart, and even more grateful to hear Julie's thoughts and feelings. I had not anticipated this when I had started the drive to her house. God truly works in mysterious ways.

A week later, Julie went to sleep on a Friday night. Joe and Laura were next to her bed. All of a sudden, both of their Labs started moaning and groaning, snuck inside their bedroom and sat on both sides of her bed, quietly looking at the dark ceiling. Julie's body shivered. Her hands lifted as if to clasp the air, and her torso briefly raised off the bed. When she dropped back on her bed, life had left her. The dogs sprinted from the room, as if they were following someone.

Joe and Laura knew then that Julie had departed to her eternal home.

* * *

I paused and let out a deep sigh. Harry knew this trip down memory lane had brought sadness to my day.

'I'm sorry for making you re-live such a sad journey, doc. I don't know how you keep doing what you do every day. It takes a special person to do that every day of your life.'

'Sometimes I wonder myself, just exactly how I keep coming back to work the next day after losses like this. It gets hard. When I hear about my patients leaving this world or when I have to recommend hospice care to someone, I feel drained. Sometimes I can't even talk about it with my wife for days. But every day, there's a new Julie, or a new Annie, or sometimes even a new Harry who needs my help. That keeps me going.'

'You know, doc, I learn from these stories. I am getting a clearer picture now as to how I want to prepare for my own journey. I can figure out roles for Susan, my kids and my pets. Thanks again for today.'

He thought for a few moments, then asked hesitantly, 'Doctor Patel, I'm feeling weaker by the day and it's hard to say how long I have. Is there any chance we could step up our times together? Like, daily?'

My schedule was a busy one, but I wanted to accommodate Harry as best I could. 'Well, my friend, I probably couldn't meet every day, but I will do my best. I do have lunchtime tomorrow free. Would you like to try for that?'

'Yes, and thanks!' Harry said. 'It seems like Julie had strong faith in God, which saw her through her battle with cancer—and through death itself. So I'd like to hear about the role of faith in dealing with dying.

'I grew up as an agnostic. I have only vague memories of going to church. I am more of a believer in a general higher power. My children all follow very eclectic spiritual beliefs. I was wondering if faith or spiritual inclination enhanced one's ability to handle the transition between life and death—the eternal journey to one's home or wherever one thinks he or she is heading.'

'I believe it does, Harry,' I said. 'Let's talk about that tomorrow. Then, for next time, I'm thinking of some patients who share a connected story that may help you. Jim and Lena. Or maybe I'll tell you about Ann.'

I paused as I recalled these gallant patients.

'Do you ever miss them?' Harry asked. 'Do you ever get used to moving on?'

'Perhaps not in this lifetime.'

Seeing the moisture in the corner of my eye, Harry remained silent.

'I was always proud of my photographic memory, Harry. I can remember almost everything I see, hear and read. That's not always good. Sometimes, I just want to close my eyes and take a deep breath and enter a trance to forget everything I ever saw or heard. There are times I lose sleep. There are times I want to take away others' pains and give away my own life in exchange. But it is the journey that I cherish.'

We sat silently for a few moments, enjoying the peace and energy of the beautiful garden. Then we bid each other goodbye and agreed to meet the following noon.

6

How the Judeo-Christian Faith
Regards Death

Even though I walk through the valley of the shadow of death,
I will fear no evil,
for you are with me;
your rod and your staff, they comfort me.

—*Psalm 23:4*

As he went home that night, Harry's mind was occupied with thoughts of Julie and her story. The pain, the debilitation and the incredible stress that her family had gone through scared him, but the strength of that amazing woman and her family, even her beloved dogs, surprised him. As he thought more about the story, he realized that faith had been the key for her to keep going in the face of what was on the horizon.

And so, he thought about his own faith. His faith had changed over the years, but now he sought to draw on it to ease the fears he felt, like Julie did. It was with thoughts about faith that his next conversation with me began.

'As you know, Harry, though I grew up as a Hindu, I went to a Catholic high school. One of my best friends was a Muslim. I lived in three different continents and in multiple cities. Still, I had not dived deeper into the post-death rituals and beliefs about death and the afterlife in different faiths until I met Ann. She inspired me to learn about cross-cultural faith.'

Harry said, 'And me, even though I was born into a Christian family in the UK, I grew up more like an agnostic. Now that I am living every day against my own mortality, I do not believe I have enough time to go back to church. However, I certainly would like to hear what you learnt about Christianity and death.'

'I do not claim to be an authority in multiple faiths. What I have learnt was from Catholic school and from my patient, Ann. Her faith was primarily focused on the Presbyterian school of theology, as her husband was a leading minister in the Westminster Church.

'Christianity's view of death and the afterlife is shaped around the fact that God became human for the sake of humanity, and was willing to die selflessly so that human beings could live eternally. The Christian God is not only the god of those who suffer, but the god who suffers with us. He went through all phases of life to demonstrate that while there is suffering in life, there is a solution too, and He came to the earth as a human being to reveal the path to salvation. All humans die, but Jesus was raised to life beyond death, and Christians believe that humans can receive everlasting life by acknowledging Jesus Christ as their saviour from the curse of sin. Death does not have the final say in Christian theology—it merely has a role.

'The death and resurrection of Christ led to two rituals: baptism and communion, which is also called the Lord's Supper or the Eucharist. By partaking of the blood and body of Christ through the ritual of the Eucharist, Christians remember Him and connect themselves with His death.

'Outside of these two common rituals, Christians have a diversity of opinions about death and dying. Not all Christians view death through the same lens. One group of believers look at death as the natural fate of human beings. They perceive Christ's resurrection as a miraculous act of God. Another school of thought views death and suffering as a punishment, linked to Adam, who brought sin and death into the world by disobeying God's commands in the Garden of Eden. Christ is the only one who can enable humanity to transcend the penalty of sin. The third view of death, according to a theologian named Soskice, is that God does not impose suffering, illness or death as punishments. Rather, death itself is the enemy that needs to be conquered.'

'This is bringing back some memories, doc,' Harry said. 'I forgot long ago what I had learnt as a child in church. Perhaps I can find solace, and a solution, somewhere in this dialogue. Maybe death and purgatory are somewhat related to the duality of existence, where the physical body remains behind, and the soul moves on. And maybe purgatory is like a suspended state in between. I remember some of this vaguely.'

'You have touched upon one of the most debated topics in Christianity. The resurrection of Christ as a physical body has created several schools of thought as far as it pertains to human beings. The evidence of the physical body of His resurrection is indicated by the fact that people could touch Him, and He still ate. But His was no ordinary body, particularly when He appeared in a room without the door opening to let Him in. So He showed that there will be a resurrection of the body, but that the body will be very special. The Bible calls this resurrected body a "glorified" body, and it promises that all believers in Christ who die physically will one day be resurrected, and their glorified bodies will rejoin their souls in heaven.'

Harry seemed incredulous. 'Wow, that would be quite a puzzle for God to sort out, wouldn't it?'

'Well, Harry,' I said, 'you're right about that, but Christians will reply that the same God who created heaven and earth from nothing, and who created human beings and animals and the laws of nature, would have no trouble reuniting a Christian's resurrected, glorified, eternal body with his or her eternal soul.'

I paused for a moment to let that sink in.

'Dante's *Divine Comedy* is perhaps the most favoured view of death and the afterlife, where large numbers of Christians, at least in the US, place heavy emphasis on the journey of the soul after death. Nevertheless, many different authorities place heavy emphasis on hell as the afterlife for non-believers and sinners. Pragmatically speaking, many preachers and missionaries put the fear of hell and the threat of God's anger at the centre of their preaching and sermons. Interestingly, the imagery of hell associated with perennial damnation, with endless burning flames and never-ending torments, is similar in Islam and Christianity.'

Harry said, 'Tell me, then, are heaven and hell actual places? I remember an uproar when Pope John Paul II commented on this.'

'Indeed, that was the case when Pope John Paul II described heaven and hell as states of the soul rather than physical places. According to his opinion, heaven is the state of the soul in communion with God and in God's presence; hell is the state of the soul away from God, alienated and separated from Him. Conservative Protestant theologians believe that heaven and hell are actual places. As far as purgatory is concerned, it is primarily a concept of Catholicism. It is the place where people who have committed sins go to cleanse themselves after death. Purgatory and its related rituals, particularly Catholic priests asking for money from relatives to exempt the dead from purgatory, led to the rise of Lutheranism. Protestant evangelical Christian theologians will tell you that the Bible does not support the concept of purgatory.'

'So, what do Hindus believe?' Harry asked.

'Harry, I will narrate the Hindu philosophy when we talk about my own beliefs on life and death. I can also say that by now, many religions have become pluralist religions, accepting some of the tenets of other faiths for their righteousness and for their right to passage to heaven after death.'

'So how do Christians prepare for death, doc?'

'In Catholicism, the sacrament of the anointing of the sick is administered to the gravely ill. Many Protestant denominations also practise some form of prayer for healing the sick.

'According to Father Joseph McGovern, Catholics believe that death is only a temporary separation that affects what people can do, but they are always capable of helping others get to heaven.

'The Catholic funeral ritual involves three phases: the vigil, the funeral liturgy itself, and communion, which connects the life and death of the deceased with the life and death of Jesus Christ. The final ritual is committal, where the body or ashes of the deceased are placed in the grave or the place of interment.

'Mass is celebrated annually for all deceased parish members on All Souls' Day. On 2 November, all members of the parish come together to pray for the dead, and meditate and reflect on death and salvation.

'Protestant death rituals are similar. There are visitations or wakes for one or two days, then a funeral in a church or a funeral home chapel, along with the committal when the body or ashes are put in the ground. Memorial services may be carried out at the burial site or another place. A typical Protestant funeral includes psalms and hymns, music, prayer, scripture readings, a eulogy or two, and a biblical message from the pastor.'

Harry nodded his understanding, then asked, 'How about other Abrahamic religions? Do others believe in the afterlife? How do their death rituals differ from us, and what makes them think that way?'

'Sure,' I agreed. 'Recent surveys have shown that a lot of American Jews believe in an afterlife, which represents an interesting resurgence in American Jewish belief.'

In Judaism, the human body is a gift from God, and even after death, it must be treated with the utmost care and respect. Even among those who believe in the afterlife, the death of a loved one is experienced and treated as a painful loss. Because Jacob tore his clothes after his son Joseph died, devoted Jews tear their clothing upon the death of a loved one.

Candles are placed around the dead body. Volunteers from a synagogue, sometimes along with family members, prepare the body for burial. They wash the body of the deceased to purify it. It is then clothed in a simple, white burial garment, usually linen, representing that there are no distinctions among people in death—all are equal before God. Until burial, the body of the deceased is guarded by a *shomer*, who stays with it and reads psalms, stories or poetry to the one who has died.

Devoted Jews are often buried in a prayer shawl. Burial, either in a simple wooden casket or directly into the ground, typically takes place within twenty-four hours or as soon as possible after death. There is no embalming or preservation of the body. There is no viewing or open-casket ceremony.

According to Jewish customs, the mourners themselves fill the grave following the lowering of the coffin. This may be done symbolically by shovelling in a small amount of earth. This is understood as a tie-breaking ritual, requiring a physical act to imprint on the body and mind the reality of death.

Cremation is forbidden for most Orthodox Jews, as they believe that the body should be allowed to decompose naturally and return to the earth from which it was made. The funeral itself can be held at the graveside, in a synagogue or in a funeral home. The funeral service is normally conducted by a rabbi or a cantor. The main elements of the short, simple ritual are the reading of prayers and psalms and the giving of eulogies for the deceased. At the end of the service, a memorial prayer is recited.

Following the Jewish funeral and burial, the mourning period begins. It is carried out in three phases. The first phase is when family members begin a period of intense mourning, known as 'sitting shiva'. 'Shiva' is Hebrew for seven; the period traditionally lasts seven days. Friends and neighbours come to sit with the mourning family, share their grief and show support. Typically, family members do not even cook, and relatives, friends and neighbours bring cooked meals.

The second phase of mourning, known as 'shloshim', or thirty, occurs in the month following the burial. Mourners do not attend social gatherings during the second period and continue to recite the *Mourner's Kaddish* daily. For those mourning the loss of a parent, this period lasts for a year after death—an expression of the unique place of a parent in the life of a Jew.

On every anniversary of the person's death, a *yahrzeit* (anniversary) candle is lit. The person's children, parents, spouse and siblings recite the *Mourner's Kaddish*, and some fast.

Sometime between the second month and a full year after a Jewish loved one's death, the tombstone is unveiled. There is a short service, the words on the tombstone are read and people often place a pebble on the grave to mark their visit. The Jewish tombstone ritual provides a space for the mourners to think about the deceased without the emotional intensity of the earlier funeral.

As far as the afterlife is concerned, Orthodox Judaism is the one that makes the most frequent reference to an afterlife. In general, up until the middle part of the past century, Jews rarely believed in an afterlife. However, with more interfaith interactions, many Jews now believe in some form of afterlife.

There are places in the Hebrew Bible that may mention the afterlife, or 'Gehinnom'. It is seen as a hell-like place where the deceased, who is not a firm believer, is sent. This place is impure and filled with death, where all individuals who oppose God's will are sent. Islam has a similar mention of a place called 'Jahannam'.

Apart from the concept of Gehinnom, the Jewish faith—particularly under the rule of the Hellenistic Seleucid empire, where Jews were forced to follow the polytheistic religions of ancient Greece and Rome—developed the idea of the resurrection of the body after death. God would establish His righteous kingdom on earth and raise the dead, so they could dwell in it. However, the Jewish belief in resurrection was significantly different than that of other faiths. In contrast to other faiths, where the belief was firmly set on disembodied souls rising to heaven, Jews at the beginning of the common era envisioned the body and soul as being resurrected together.

Between the thirteenth and the eighteenth centuries, there was another turn in the Jewish belief system of the duality of existence, where more and more people started believing in a soul that survived death without a body. This followed the Greek belief in an immortal soul that left the body upon death. But these Jews rejected the idea of resurrection.

Reincarnation, despite always being a minority view, is most often seen in Jewish mysticism or Kabbalah; in Hasidism—a form of pietistic Orthodox Judaism; and in the Yiddish literature of diaspora Jews in Europe. These mystics of Judaism believe that a soul progressively goes through cycles of rebirth to cleanse sins and through meditation—or the practice of Kabballah, through multiple reincarnations.

These are just a couple of examples of belief systems that include resurrection, reincarnation or some form of afterlife.

Harry paused to think. Whatever school of thought he considered, there was the glimmer of hope of an afterlife to think through. What form or shape it would take, he still didn't know. But the thought comforted him, that the world's religions agreed there was no darkness at the end.

'Wow,' Harry sighed. 'You know so much more about religion than I do. I guess it's both comforting and sobering to think that there may indeed be some form of afterlife for us all.'

I agreed with Harry. Then I said, 'That's probably enough for today, isn't it, Harry?'

Harry nodded. 'Yes, doc. It required a lot of focus to follow what you said, and I admit I'm feeling a bit tired.'

'So, next time, do you want to continue exploring religious views of death and the afterlife, or would you prefer to hear Ann's story?'

'Oh, I'm ready for another story. I seem to gain strength and encouragement from hearing about your patients. I want to hear about Ann.'

'Absolutely, my friend. Ann will inspire you, as she did me. She never looked at suffering with agony. In every challenge, she saw the light, and she saw blessing; she looked at suffering as an opportunity to be a witness for the Almighty.'

'Wow,' was all Harry could say.

I had learnt a lot from Ann.

'Is she—sorry—was she from Rock Hill?'

'Yes indeed, and perhaps your wife, Susan, may have met her. Ann was a volunteer at the hospital. And her daughter works at the ER now and—how can I forget—her husband, Shelton, is a senior pastor at the largest church in Rock Hill. What a love story! They met in kindergarten and had been with each other except for a few years in school.'

'I will look forward to hearing about Ann,' Harry said.

We set a time for our next meeting and bid each other goodbye. As he walked away, I noticed that Harry was moving more slowly than last time.

7

The Beginning of the End
or the End of the Beginning?

There is no death! The stars go down to rise upon some other shore,
And bright in heaven's jewelled crown, they shine forevermore.

—J.L. McCreery

'Hi, Dr Patel, this is Connie. Mum is having severe pain in her legs, like charley horses. She was tossing and turning in bed the whole night.'

'Oh, Connie,' I replied. 'I just saw her last month, and everything seemed fine. She looked the best since I have seen her as a patient.' I was not overly concerned, but I have learnt to always listen to my patients. They know their bodies better than anyone else. 'Let me have a quick look at her, though. When can you bring her in? Tomorrow morning?' I did not want to take any chances.

'You know, Dr Patel, Mum will never verbalize her suffering. She wants to remain a positive witness for Jesus in this life.

She will downplay all her suffering and pain. You will need to dig deep with her. I am getting worried about her.'

A few months back, after intensive treatment followed by a bone marrow transplant, Ann had been declared free of her leukaemia and had just started moving on with her life.

The next morning, Ann came to the clinic along with her pastor husband, Shelton, and Connie, their daughter, who had called the previous day. Ann's neck muscles were visibly tight and her lips pursed. She looked somewhat frail. Her lips were bright red, and her cheeks had a red tinge. In addition, she wore enough make-up to hide her fatigue from sleepless nights. Her fists were tightly clenched, and her knees hugged together as if she were in deep discomfort.

Her genuine smile was trying to conceal her suffering.

'Hello, Ann!' I greeted. 'Ms Eternal Optimist!'

'Eternally faithful, Dr Patel. It is you who is the eternal optimist, and I am the eternally faithful witness.' Ann wanted me to learn the difference between faith and optimism.

I always enjoyed eclectic conversations with her about my confused terminology, having lived in three continents and twelve cities in the short span of fifteen years.

'Tell me what's going on. Connie is worried about your leg cramps and you not sleeping well. I can see your knees are tightly locked. How long has this been going on?'

'Well, on and off for the last couple of weeks. You know, since I returned from the hospital, I have been doing so much at home, running around after my grandchildren! I know I should have taken it easy. I've learnt my lesson, I promise. I will listen to my body from now on.'

'Well, since your last visit just a few weeks back did not reveal any problems, I don't believe we should be terribly concerned. But prevention is always better than cure. Let me examine you briefly and do another blood count. Then we will figure out our next step.'

I examined her thoroughly. There weren't any obvious signs to be worried about. I saw no sign of leukaemia, such as oral ulcers or bleeding spots. I attributed her symptoms to a combination of her speedy recovery from leukaemia and her bone marrow cells crowding the large bones of her lower limb. If it had happened faster than usual it could have led to the leg pains. Her blood count was even better than on her last visit. All blood cell lines were normal.

'Everything looks good,' I was happy to report. 'You may be right, Ann. You may have overdone it. Be careful and listen to your body.' I reassured her that nothing seemed to be amiss and that the leg pains were probably due to overproduction of bone marrow stem cells or overexertion.

Connie jumped in. 'Dr Patel, I know you know your subject well. I know my mum well enough, though. She is not herself. She always will downplay her symptoms. Lately, she has been blissfully silent. I can see she's in pain and yet she is smiling more than ever. Would you mind checking her weekly? I'm just worried.'

'Okay,' Ann jumped in. 'I'll be honest. Connie is right. I am having this very unusual physical unease, yet I feel calm inside. My body seems to be going down and my spirit seems to be moving upwards. But I haven't been able to sleep at night due to cramps.'

'Do you want some pain meds?'

'Oh, no, I don't want pain meds. I can live with this. I just thought I would share this weird feeling that I can't figure out.'

'Okay,' I said. 'Let's see you weekly and monitor this.'

'Thank God.' Connie appeared relieved.

Although I didn't detect anything unusual in Ann's pain, she did. Maybe she was instinctively aware of something that all my tests had missed. She had picked up on the skill of listening to her body, and it was telling her that all was not well.

What I did detect was that Ann herself seemed different, but I couldn't quite figure out how. It wasn't her attitude—she was not depressed or overly anxious. All she wanted to do was affirm what she thought was happening in her body. No matter how much I reassured her, I could tell that she took the leg pains seriously.

Ann continued her weekly appointments for the next month. She had undergone a bone marrow transplant four months earlier and, so far, everything was proceeding as expected for her recovery.

Outside my clinic, fall was in full swing and the day had brought the season's first cold air. The soil was covered with freshly fallen yellow leaves from the trees. The sun hid behind an overcast sky. The prematurely chilly winter air brought in an unusual gloom. Ann was the last patient scheduled for the day. Today would be her last weekly appointment—I wanted to switch her to a monthly follow-up schedule again.

As usual, Shelton and their daughter Connie had accompanied her. Ann looked good. Her skin had an excellent colour, and her face was bright. She carried the same smile. But behind that smile, I detected a bit of detachment. It was as if Ann had lost interest in everything outside of her faith.

By now, her leg pains and flu-like symptoms had disappeared. I asked whether she was feeling anything unusual, and she denied any abnormal symptoms after the leg pains had disappeared. Again, I thoroughly examined her and did not find any abnormalities.

I remarked, 'Another month has gone by, and you still seem fine! Let me take a look at the blood work and then you can go home.'

It was the last week of October. This was likely Ann's last office visit of the year. With each passing month, the chances of her leukaemia returning were lessening.

Yet Ann was dispassionately quiet. 'No problem, doctor,' she replied faintly. 'We can wait for the blood count results.' She was much more reticent than during any of her other visits. Was there something she was concerned about? I would ask her after we reviewed her blood work.

There was a knock on the door. My lab specialist, April, was waiting outside.

'Come in, April!' I said jovially.

'Dr Patel, could I talk to you outside for a minute?'

'Sure.' When I had left the room and closed the door behind me, April handed me Ann's blood report. It took less than a second to realize that something was very wrong. I had to ask the usual screening questions. 'Are you sure you had a good sample? Are you sure the specimen wasn't overly diluted? Maybe blood clotted and that is why the tests look abnormal.'

I could think of a million reasons for what I saw in the report, except for the most obvious and most painful. April shook her head at all of my queries. That meant that the blood results could only have come from one thing.

Walking back into the examining room was difficult. No amount of experience ever prepares doctors for some of the conversations they must have with patients. It felt even harder because, just a few minutes ago, I had reassured Ann and Shelton and their daughter Connie that nothing was wrong.

I began cautiously. 'Ann, your blood count is not entirely normal. Your white blood cell count has dropped somewhat, and so have your platelets. Although there isn't an overly pronounced drop, it is still significant, and this worries me.'

Connie immediately understood the words I had left unstated.

'Is her leukaemia back?'

Connie was visibly upset. Her initial reaction was just like mine—utter disbelief. I glanced at Ann's husband. Shelton's face had fallen, and he seemed to have suddenly entered a state of severe melancholy.

Tears started forming in everyone's eyes, including my own. I did not have to verbalize my answer to Connie's question.

'Now what?' Connie broke the silence. 'Are there any options left?'

'Let's plan for the next step before we lose time,' I said as calmly as I could. 'Her leukaemia may be returning. I want to send her back to Gary, my dear friend and colleague, who may have better answers. He can explore allogeneic transplant.'

'Bone marrow transplant again?' Connie gasped. 'Isn't that very hard on the body?'

'Yes, but it may be our only way forward,' I said.

'How soon can we get going?'

'Let me make the call.'

'Hey, Gary, this is Kashyap. I hate to disrupt you at the end of the day. I need your help.'

'Anytime for you, my friend. How is your sweet wife doing?' I was not sure if Gary could sense the tremor in my voice.

'Do you remember my patient, Ann?'

'Of course! Is her leukaemia back? I suspected that beast might come back.'

'Yes.' I did not have any more energy left.

'Send her to Greenville right away,' Gary said. 'I'll arrange for her admission to the same floor and room she had before.'

'They will be on their way shortly.'

Ann's life had turned upside down again. For the last ten months, her life had been lived between the hospital, chemotherapy centre and infusion centres. Her body had been pricked countless times in the hope of finding answers. Then she was declared in remission. She had just started regaining control of her life.

She was admitted to the same hospital room with the garden view. But this time she had a strange feeling of detachment.

Everything had changed: her approach to life, her attitude towards life and her relationship with the world. She sensed that she was on the last leg of her journey on this planet. All she wanted was some time to allow her family to accept whatever outcome was barrelling her way.

Ann received intensive chemotherapy to control her leukaemia so she could enter a second remission. It didn't matter how long or short the remission was—it just had to be long enough for the doctors to complete the bone marrow transplant.

No matter what her doctors said, she was confident that nothing was going to save her at this point. The only reason she tolerated the harsh and desperate therapy was for the sake of her family. While she had accepted that she would soon be in the presence of Jesus, Shelton and Connie had not. Ann did not want them living with the guilt that they didn't do everything possible to save her.

With each passing day, Ann became weaker. Leukaemic cells were invading each of her organs despite the chemo bombardment. She finished her chemotherapy on Valentine's Day—exactly one year after her original diagnosis.

But her condition worsened rapidly. Now she needed a blood and platelet transfusion every week. Her lungs were covered in angry leukaemic cells, and she had difficulty breathing. Between the infections caused by her demolished immune system and lung blood vessels clogged with leukaemia cells, doctors could no longer tell what was hindering her breathing.

Many specialists examined her, and each had a different opinion. But they all still had one thing in common. They established that her leukaemia had become fastidious and was growing more rapidly each day. Even a transplant by the world's best doctors in the world's best hospital wouldn't stop the relentless march of the leukaemic blasts now. Everyone—from doctors to nurses to Ann's family to Ann herself—wanted an answer:

What had happened? What had gone wrong? Why had the leukaemia returned with such a vengeance?

'Hello, Dr Patel. This is Connie. I apologize for calling you on your cell phone, but we need your help.'

Her voice was broken. Something weighed heavily on her mind.

'No problem, Connie. You can call me anytime on my cell phone. What can I do for you?'

'Mum is not doing well. She has been in the hospital for the last several weeks. After her last chemotherapy, she has gone downhill quickly. She is struggling for every breath. I am not sure if we are on the right path. I know what lies ahead for us.'

She started sobbing.

'I will be on my way soon,' I assured her.

'She is in room 307. She will be going for a bone marrow test soon. Otherwise, we should all be in her room.'

I reached Ann's room in the late afternoon. Her body appeared frail. Visible portions of her skin were covered in raised red spots. It was difficult to say if these were leukaemia cells clustered under her skin or if she was bleeding under the skin. Her neck muscles were prominent. While her face still bore that blissful smile, her eyes looked sunken.

She had to stop between sentences to catch her breath. She looked anxious, as if impatient to pack her bags and move along. The look on her face, her feeble voice and her body slowly wasting away all pointed to her readiness to exit this life for the next.

My friend, who was treating Ann at the hospital, Dr Gary Spitzer, joined us shortly. Before he could begin, Shelton asked permission to say a prayer. We held hands together, surrounding her bed. It was indeed a divine scene to see an Australian Jewish oncologist, a southern Episcopalian pulmonologist and an Indian Hindu oncologist hold hands while a Westminster Protestant pastor prayed for an eternally faithful patient, who always saw herself as a witness for Jesus regardless of her pain. For a few moments, we all forgot why we were there.

Finally, Gary broke the silence. 'The news isn't good. Almost 90 per cent of the marrow space has been replaced with cancer cells. There is no space left for normal marrow maturation. I wish I could give you some hope, but at this point, I think being completely honest is best. I don't believe Ann will make it for more than a few weeks. I think the best thing now is to consider what she wants, rather than think about what we want for her.'

As Gary spoke, he had none of his usual enthusiasm. Ann had touched the heart of everyone she had come in contact with, including this grizzled old oncologist. He was extremely sorry that he had to deliver this news.

'You mean it's over?' Connie burst out. 'No, that can't be! There must be some procedure or hospital that can save her!'

Gary looked Connie in the eye sympathetically, his voice firm but gentle. 'I wish I had something different to tell you, Connie. I'm afraid that at some point we all are going to die of one thing or another. If there were any place we could send her, neither Dr Patel nor I would hesitate for a second. But at this point, even a miracle is impossible. The best thing now is not to waste a moment that we still have with Ann and do whatever she wishes for her last days.'

Gary was usually not one to talk like a philosopher; the family realized how serious and resolved he was.

'Can you at least tell us one thing? What happened? What went wrong with the leukaemia?'

This question is common among everyone whose cancer suddenly returns after remission.

My friend was patient and kind. 'Leukaemic cells are very intelligent,' Gary explained. 'Ann, your latest bone marrow report shows multiple new mutations, indicating that your leukaemia cells have evolved into a much more aggressive form, which is also very resistant and fastidious. They have developed MDR, or multiple drug resistance, genes. We still don't know how it works or how to prevent it, but it causes the cells to become immune to the chemo poisons that had destroyed them in the past. Scientists are still working every day to try to prevent these genes from forming, but we are still miles from a solution.'

Gary's answer finally told us what had happened with Ann. Somewhere, some leukaemia cells had survived the chemotherapy bombardment. These survivors had developed a mutation that had made them more aggressive and also resistant to chemotherapy. That was why none of our regimens could work any more, and also why we couldn't get Ann into a second remission for the bone marrow transplant.

Ann quietly asked, 'Can I go home today? And if so, can I go now?' This was the first time Ann had intervened in the discussion. She continued, 'I want to spend my last few days at my own home, where I have spent the last three decades. I have known for the past few months that my time is coming to an end. I have no regrets.'

'Yes, of course,' Gary replied. 'Let me coordinate all the arrangements for hospice care for you at home. And I'll send a nurse to your home to help ensure that you are comfortable.'

Gary started making arrangements immediately. He didn't want Ann to lose a single second of the time she had left. Ann returned home the next day, uncertain whether her journey was ending or beginning. It was probably a blend of both. In spite of difficulty breathing and lack of oxygen in her body, her mind was still sharp and clear. She had never resisted the idea of dying and leaving this world; she knew quite well that she would be going to join her heavenly Father.

Winter, spring, summer, fall and another winter had passed since her first diagnosis. Last winter, the family was hoping for a cure. Now, the family was simply hoping for minimal suffering as Ann's condition deteriorated. She had lost a lot of weight. Her body's normal tissues were losing the battle against the ever-replicating leukaemia cells.

But no matter how much havoc leukaemia wreaked on Ann's physical body, it was not able to break her will and faith in God and His love. No matter what end Ann came to, she would be the victor. Neither the suffering nor the apprehension of physical death was able to remove the wonderful smile that even her weak and wrinkled face wore. Even in her own suffering, she saw the Lord's hand at work and believed that He would bring about His perfect will for His glory.

Ann's suffering in the last few days had been increasingly obvious. Even walking a few steps was strenuous. Shelton had positioned Ann's bed against the wall so she could enjoy the beauty of the backyard. Her frailty no longer allowed her to stand on the deck.

Even in the harshness of winter, the dry and barren leafless trees couldn't shake her belief in the Lord's care for all things. She still saw the occasional squirrel scamper over the dry branches, and a bird that must have been lost en route to Florida make its home there. These sights reminded her of the Creator's presence. He had granted life to a bird where logically there should have been none. Its voice reminded her of the voice of the Creator that she now heard everywhere. As night fell, she could see faint lights from distant stars, reminding her that God's presence spanned many galaxies, reaching millions of light-years away.

On 3 March, I paid a visit to Ann to see how she was doing and if I could help ease her pain in any way.

'Hello, Ann. How are you feeling today?' I greeted her.

She smiled up at me and said, 'Bodily, you can see I'm quite weak and fragile, Dr Patel. But mentally, I'm still the same woman I've always been! If anything, now I'm finally at ease and comfortable with the direction God has decided to take me.

I think He wants me by His side sooner rather than later. At least I'm no longer confused about how much longer I have.'

Although noticeably enfeebled, she was still able to compose words and express herself clearly.

'Are you in any discomfort? Do you hurt?' I was trying to pinpoint any symptoms I could help her with. 'Please don't hesitate to ask for any pain medicines. It is okay to ask for help. I know we now have limited time with you. As much as I wish you could have stayed with us, I agree that the Lord has different plans for you. He wants you to go home to Him, and sooner rather than later.'

We talked further about our views of the afterlife. Ann maintained her solid belief that Jesus Christ had secured eternal salvation for her. She knew that throughout her earthly journey, He loved her and was with her. She accepted that leukaemia was part of God's sovereign plan for her life. She had no regrets and was ready for the Lord's angels to come and take her to her heavenly home. Her steady faith was an incredible example to me.

As we wrapped up our visit, the effects of Ann's most recent morphine dose were making themselves known as her speech slowed and her voice grew weaker.

'Ann, can I be of any help to you in this transition between life and what comes after?'

'Oh, Dr Patel, you have truly been a godsend,' Ann smiled as she took my hand in hers. 'You have made this journey so much easier for me and my family. You've done all you can for me now. May God bless you! I look forward to seeing you someday in heaven with our Holy Father.'

These were Ann's final words for me. I said my last goodbye to the lady who had so touched the most inner part of my soul.

Time passed quickly after that. Ann got weaker and weaker, and her often-vacant eyes would stare at the sky outside the window almost constantly, as if they saw something the others couldn't. She spoke of heavenly music the others couldn't hear.

Finally, it was Shelton who realized what was happening. Ann was seeking permission to begin her journey to heaven. He asked all the family members, including all her daughters, sons-in-law, son and grandchildren, to come into her room. Even the family dog accompanied them.

They all held hands as he began a prayer.

He then slowly took her hands into his own, kissed her on her cheek, and said gently, 'Ann, I love you. I know you can't wait to be in heaven with Jesus. You have been my light and my joy for so many years. You were by my side in rough and good times. There are countless reasons for me to want to say, "Please don't leave me here by myself."

'But there is just one reason to say that you have my permission to move on so you can be in God's presence. The reason is that I know you are going to Jesus, our Saviour, and any such reason trumps all that I can offer. I love you, sweetheart. All of us love you with all our hearts. Your passing will leave a permanent hole in our hearts. We are going to miss you so much. But whenever you're ready, it is okay for you to move on.

'I will miss you always, and we will be reunited in God's heavenly kingdom. I can't wait to join you and behold the glory and beauty of our Lord Jesus.'

One after the other, all the family members came to say their goodbyes to Ann. As hard as it was to do, they at least were thankful that the Lord had allowed them the time and opportunity to do so. The family dog sat silently nearby, maintaining a quiet vigil by her side.

Shelton's words made a monumental difference. After everyone had said their goodbyes, Ann appeared relaxed. Her vacant eyes no longer searched the skies. Her breathing slowed. The next day, Ann slept most of the time. She did not appear to be in discomfort.

Two days later, on the bright sunny morning of 7 March, Shelton and Connie were sitting beside Ann's bed. The dog was sleeping on the floor and the grandchildren were in another room. Ann's breathing grew heavier and deeper than usual. She was slowly slipping into a coma.

Suddenly, they both saw Ann's face brighten as if she saw something heading her way. She opened her eyes, lifted her head towards the ceiling and raised her hands in the air. Her face was serene. It was almost as if Jesus were reaching down to her and she was trying to take His hand. Shelton helped lift her up, fully aware that the time had arrived for Ann to depart from this world. Though he couldn't see anything, he felt the presence of Jesus in the room.

Ann opened her mouth, offered one final smile, and whispered, 'Oh Lord! I am coming to Your kingdom!'

Shelton felt a sudden jerk, followed by heaviness in his hands. The life had finally crept out of Ann's body. Her soul and spirit were now with the angels, who were taking her to be with her Lord Jesus, leaving the lifeless body behind in the hands of her loved one.

Within a few days, Ann's body was buried. The soul and spirit that had graced and brightened the lives of so many, including my own, had left the earth and moved on to heaven. She left behind not just a body, but an imprint on the hearts of everyone with whom she had come in contact. Churchgoers, volunteers, nurses, doctors and family alike grieved. During the visitation, everyone in the room remembered Ann's deep love for people and her absolute assurance in the promises of God.

* * *

I ended Ann's story there. As if he had been holding his breath, Harry slowly exhaled. He looked and sounded sad. 'I hope my departure is as good as Ann's,' he said. 'Do most Christians believe what she believed? About angels coming to escort them to heaven?'

'Well, according to the Bible, Jesus told of a faithful believer who died and was carried to heaven by the angels,' I replied. 'And those who believe in Him and His teachings believe as Ann did.'

Harry asked, 'Doc, how do you keep doing this?'

'Well, my friend, people and friends like you inspire me to keep doing what I do. I believe in learning. I am a lifelong learner. And, of course, I want to apply what I learn to help patients along this journey.'

Harry paused. His body was bearing the damage of the cancer within him, but his resolve was strengthening. Though the burden of his impending mortality hung upon him every moment, the stories of these patients were helping him overcome it. Knowing that others had faced what he now did, and had still found a way to thrive before the end came was his newfound strength in the shadow of his disease. The strength of Ann's faith had protected both her and her family. And for him, that was a lesson well learnt—that his family could be guarded with the strength of faith. And though he'd never gone to church as much as Shelton and Ann had, it did not mean that his faith was any less strong than theirs.

He drew a breath.

'Tomorrow, doc?' Harry asked. 'I may have just a month or two, or just a few weeks. Who knows for sure? But you're helping me prepare . . . myself, as well as my family. I need to make lots of decisions, and soon.'

'Sure, my friend,' I said. 'How about two o'clock tomorrow? I can have Dr Gor see a couple of my other patients while we talk. I'm thinking of two individuals whose stories were interconnected in many ways. And they brought me some of the most intense, but most rewarding, experiences of my life.'

8

Preparing to Soar

And when I, at last, must throw off this frail covering,
Which I have worn for three score years and ten,
On the brinks of the grave, I'll not seek to keep hovering,
Nor my thread wish to spin over again;
But my face in the glass I'll serenely survey,
And with smiles count each wrinkle and furrow;
As this old work out stuff which is a threadbare today,
May become everlasting tomorrow.

—J. Collins

Beep . . . beep . . . beep!

My pager interrupted my Friday evening.

I wasn't supposed to be on call, and we were getting ready to attend a wedding reception for the daughter of one of my best friends. Answering a page was the last thing I wanted to do.

'Are you ready, Kashyap?' asked Alpa, my dear wife.

'You look very beautiful in this sari,' I replied. 'And your hair looks gorgeous!'

My pager went off again. Alpa gave me a death glare. 'If you respond to that pager, I will throw it away this time. Didn't you tell me you weren't on call tonight?'

'I did. I don't know why my service keeps paging me. Maybe my partner isn't responding, or his battery died and they're calling me. Let me check.'

The message was, 'Please call James Borg on 803000000. He is aware you are not on call. Has a special request to call him.'

'Let me see what's happening,' I told Alpa. 'John Borg wants me to call him—don't know why.'

John Borg was waiting for my call. I knew John personally and professionally, and I knew he wouldn't interrupt without due cause. His mum, Lily, had been my patient for the past year.

'Nana just fell into a coma,' John told me. 'I think she's ready to start her journey to heaven. We all are ready for her too. The entire family and the hospice nurse are with her. She is breathing very slowly.'

'I hope you don't plan on calling 911 or taking her to the hospital,' I said. 'I remember having this discussion when we decided to call home hospice care for her. She didn't want to die in the hospital.'

I was trying to get John to wrap up the call, so Alpa and I could leave for the wedding. In my profession, calls like these were a daily occurrence, and as heart-rending as each call of this nature was, if I didn't allow myself some freedom to be with my family, I would never be able to continue in this line of work.

'No, that's not the case, doctor. We all know she's here with us for maybe a few more hours—if we're lucky, maybe one or two days. She's quite restless and keeps mumbling your name. I'm not sure if she is reflecting her desire for closure.'

I looked at my wife's anxious face. In situations like this, my patients have to come first. My wife could read the decision in my face before I said it. 'Honey, I need to leave. I'm so sorry,' I said.

'I can't join you at the wedding. Please forgive me. Call your friend to drive you. I have to go.'

I rushed to the Westminster Towers senior living centre, where Lily had been living for the last several months. I had seen her multiple times in recent weeks as she went downhill. She was like a legend to me—a brilliant southern belle who was still as flirtatious and romantic as ever, even at the age of eighty.

Her struggle with multiple myeloma had been a success story in the initial months of her treatment. But that had changed when the cancer had eventually returned. I remembered Christmas a few weeks back, when I had visited her at John's house. Knowing then that her life was limited to a matter of months, perhaps even weeks, John had asked me to join them for their Christmas Day family lunch as a surprise to her.

I gathered my composure as I parked next to the beautiful Westminster church and walked towards Nana's private assisted-living apartment. The long hallway's plush carpet muffled the sounds of my footsteps. Up ahead, her apartment door was open a crack.

As I entered, I saw Nana lying on the bed, breathing and sighing heavily. I could hear her breath rattling through her mouth.

'Come in, Dr Patel,' John said. 'I can't thank you enough for taking the time to come and see her.' He guided me to a chair next to her bed. He looked tired and weak from many days of visits between his work, his own treatment, his family and looking after Nana. He was wearing a mask and a cap to cover his bald head, which was yet to recover from chemotherapy hair loss. It was distressing for me to see two people who were so close to me both struggling with cancer: one who had accepted her fate and the other desperately trying to battle it with chemotherapy.

Lily was surrounded by her two daughters and sons-in-law, her two sons, and some of her grandkids. She lay in bed, wrapped in a blanket. Her eyeballs were rolling behind her closed eyelids.

While physically she looked comfortable, with minimal traces of pain, she seemed to struggle with spiritual pain, almost as if she wanted to leave for heaven but something was preventing her exit. John gently drew me closer to her bed as he whispered in her ear.

'Nana, Dr Patel is here. I know you are longing to see him. You kept asking about him, and now you are back in a deep sleep. Look, he's here.'

I gently moved closer to her and took her hand in mine.

'Lily, I am here. I knew you wanted to see me before you left. We all are here now—three generations of your family are with you. We all love you, and we give you our permission to leave us whenever you're ready. We will miss you dearly. But we also know that God wants you at His side.'

She gently opened her eyes and looked at me. Her beautiful smile briefly replaced her groans as, for a few seconds, her breath stopped rattling. I felt her hand trying to move upwards between my clasped palms. She wanted to sit up. I placed my hand behind her shrivelled back. John and his daughter Laura moved closer to help, and the three of us gently propped Lily up to a sitting position.

I couldn't believe what I heard next.

'Dr Patel, my dear son . . . I am glad you are here. I was waiting for you,' Lily said. 'I could feel and hear all of the rest of my kindred. But I would have been in terrible pain . . . to leave without seeing and bidding you goodbye with one last hug. I remember . . . I never left your office without a hug every time. How can I leave this world . . . without giving you one final hug?'

'Lily,' I spoke gently, 'that is why I am here. I know you are about to leave us. We will all be sad and will miss you.'

'Looks like your soul is ready to join your Creator,' I continued. 'We give you our permission to leave. We do not want your physical body to suffer any more. Please move on whenever you are ready.'

I looked around at everyone else; they all nodded in sorrowful agreement.

Suddenly I felt a jolting sensation in my hands. Not just me, but all three of us—John, Laura and I—felt the jolt for a brief second. Then something heavy fell into my arms. It was the lifeless, mortal remains of Lily.

She had moved on.

Gently, we eased her body back down on the bed. The hospice nurse came closer, sensing what had happened. She placed a blanket to cover Lily's body and part of her face.

Laura's husband, Randy, broke the silence. 'We can't thank you enough,' he said to me. 'I'm not sure I will ever see or hear of this type of graceful closure again in my lifetime. Thanks for doing this for us. Thanks for being who you are.'

I addressed everyone in the room. 'I wish I could stay longer. I feel privileged and honoured to have shared such a miraculous experience with you. I want to echo what Randy said. I don't think I will ever have a similar experience again in this lifetime. Thank you for allowing me to attend her last moments. I will see you all at the viewing and funeral.'

With a heavy heart, I returned home. Alpa was not back. I turned on the lights, went out to sit on the patio swing, and looked out at the dark night. Above me, I saw a shooting star.

* * *

'Oh my,' Harry exhaled softly. 'Doc, you are amazing. No wonder Susan trusts you with her life, and mine too. How did John take it? Not his mother's demise, but her waiting for you and addressing you as if you were her child? And, above all, leaving her mortal remains in your hands?'

'Well, Harry, John is the main character in our next story,' I said.

'Well, I'm still trying to envision her dying in your arms with her own son wearing a mask. Was he on chemotherapy? Did you treat him too?'

'Yes, John was in treatment too. But, no, I did not treat him.'

Before Harry could respond, he nearly doubled up with a sudden coughing fit. Eventually, the cough subsided, but his face was pale as he swallowed and took a few deep, cautious breaths.

Suddenly he clutched his side. 'Oh!' he almost screamed. 'I may have sprained my chest muscle. My right side . . .'

I reached out for him. Harry may have cracked a rib, perhaps due to an underlying cancer spot. I had a hunch that his cancer had already spread to his bones, but I needed to confirm my hunch.

'Harry, you may have ruptured or injured your rib muscles. However, to be sure, I want a scan of your chest and lungs to ensure that there is no cancer in your bones.'

'Doc, I've made it clear—I do not want to take a step back in the hospital or do any more tests.'

'We need to know about it to help us understand how to manage your care and your pain better,' I persisted.

I kept a hand on his shoulder, hoping to steady and reassure him.

Harry said, 'We already know this rotten beast is starting to take over my body.' In reality, Harry had used an expletive instead of 'rotten'.

'Pardon my language,' he hastened to add. 'I'm probably one of your worst patients when I'm in pain.' He was embarrassed about his choice of words, although cancer did deserve the adjective.

His body was now bearing the pain of his disease. But mentally, he was beginning to come to terms with his disease, and he knew that his time was limited. He had no interest in losing sight of what he sought to accomplish and why he was going through these daily talks.

With that in mind, he steeled his resolve. 'I am not interested in knowing how far or fast it's growing. I just need something to help me with the pain.'

'Sure. Let me prescribe something that will ease your pain right away. You can take one tablet every four to six hours as needed.'

I wrote out a prescription, and we set a meeting time for early the next week.

Harry rose slowly from his chair and shuffled alongside me as I walked with him from the garden.

I could tell he was growing weaker by the day.

That weekend, shortly after dinner, Harry and Susan drove to the Laser High Soaring Club near their home. The club had been a source of camaraderie and fun since they had joined. As a respected instructor, Harry had mentored many of the younger pilots and shared a close friendship with the owners, George and Edith. Harry planned to tell them of his illness and make a special request.

He opened the conversation in his usual good-natured fashion, then explained his illness and the prognosis in a simple but eloquent manner. The silence and subsequent mood shift made clear that their old friends were startled and saddened by the news.

'Would you like me to take you up in the glider?' George asked.

Harry turned to Susan. 'Thanks. I appreciate your thoughtfulness, but my last flight needs to be with Susan.'

Susan's eyes filled with tears, but she managed a smile. How she loved this man!

Harry turned to George. 'I would like you to take me up one last time, though, George,' he said. 'After I die. Would you spread my ashes over my home soaring site?'

'I can do that,' George replied softly.

'I don't want you to make a big fuss about it. I don't want a service or anything. Just take me up and let my ashes go in the wind. Who knows, maybe you'll beat the record for hitting the X.'

Although Harry had already discussed his wishes with Susan, the discussion made her chest tighten. Harry had joked about hitting the X, but her sense of humour was sapped today. Besides, she didn't want to think about Harry's ashes landing on the airfield X the pilots used for target practice.

'Make every moment count,' Susan told herself. She buried her desperation as the evening settled into a casual conversation about gliding. Like every day since Harry's diagnosis, time slipped through her fingers, and it was time to leave.

Outside in the parking lot, George hugged Harry, then Susan. 'Harry was clear about what he wants. How about you? What do you want?'

The weight of everyone's gaze weighed on Susan's shoulders as answers to the question soared through her head. She pursed her lips to frame her thoughts and control the building emotions. The days and weeks since Harry's diagnosis had been an emotional roller coaster. She couldn't imagine how she would manage his death, let alone the services after he was gone. However, she was certain of one thing.

'I want a small service with friends and family,' she said.

Harry shook his head. 'No, there's . . .'

'You don't have a say in this. You'll be dead,' George scolded his friend with a subtle smile on his lips.

Susan blinked and then turned to Harry as both dread and empowerment warred within her. 'He's right. You don't have a say in this. We're having a small service.'

'We'll help you with the arrangements. I'll make a few test runs to work out the best way to make the drop,' George said.

Harry was pensive for a moment. Susan could tell he was working through the decision.

As George opened the car door for Susan, he asked Harry, 'Could we throw a going-away party for you?'

Unflappable Harry suddenly seemed stuck for a response. He loved parties. However, the stiff-lipped Brit didn't want to be the reason for the party.

'I like the idea!' Susan said. 'A wake before you die.'

Harry opened the driver's door. 'I don't know. I need to think about it. I'll get back to you.'

During the thirty-minute drive home, Harry decided to agree to the party as long as it was an upbeat event. To ensure the celebration didn't turn to grief, Harry composed the invitations. For friends who knew Harry's prognosis, the meaning was clear. To acquaintances who didn't know Harry was sick, the invitation suggested that Harry planned to move from the area. In fact, as far as he was concerned, he was 'moving'.

When they reached home, Harry began to exit the car when he screamed. 'Susan, help me! I've twisted my back!' he exclaimed as he writhed in pain.

'Oh my! This is not good.' Susan knew exactly what was happening. Even though Harry thought he had sprained his back, Susan knew this was a sign of the cancer invading his spine and bones. 'Let's go to the hospital or call Dr Patel. I am worried for you, Harry.'

'Darling, I do not want to go to the hospital. I have already checked that box. Dr Patel very well suspects that my cancer has spread to my bones, and I already had this discussion with him. No use bothering him or calling him on the weekend. Let him have some time off too. Would you please help me get in the house and then get the pain meds for me?'

'So, you already had pain in your bones, and Dr Patel put you on narcotics? You did not tell me! I'm your wife, and I'm worried about you!'

'Honey, nothing will change what I have to go through. I don't want to burden you with small things that I can handle myself. You are already struggling with the whole situation. Let me offload some of this burden from your shoulders. Please bring me water and the meds now.'

Over the next couple of days, Harry's pain worsened. Finally, he agreed to let Susan reach out to me for help.

She looked quite distressed. She no longer bothered with make-up, and her bloodshot eyes made her look like she'd aged decades in the past few months.

'Kashyap, Harry is hurting a lot in his mid-back, and he is not willing to do anything beyond taking pain meds. He's almost hunched over, and I'm worried his backbone may have weakened from the cancer. Can you do something? Do you know what would be causing this?'

'Susan,' I began, 'it looks like the lung cancer cells are invading his bones. The cancer seems to be eroding or, in plain language, eating his bones one at a time. This, in turn, seems to be causing pressure on the nerves passing between two adjacent vertebrae, leading to irritation and pain.

'Ideally, I would recommend radiation, which I know is not an option, since Harry has decided against any intervention. The only other thing we can do is get a rigid back brace to provide support to his back—and a walking stick to lift some of the weight off as he stands or walks.'

Susan nodded slowly, hesitantly. 'Sounds like the only viable option,' she said, and agreed to convince Harry to at least try it. 'Let me see if Harry's pain has eased.'

9

Many Bodies, One Soul

Life is a journey.
Death is a return to earth.
The universe is like an inn.
The passing years are like dust.
Regard this phantom world
As a star at dawn, a bubble in a stream,
A flash of lightning in a summer cloud,
A flickering lamp—a phantom—and a dream.

—Gautam Buddha

I did not hear from either Harry or Susan until Tuesday, when Harry showed up for our lunch date. He hobbled with his new cane and was in obvious discomfort as we made our way slowly to the golden dome in the garden. The sun was shining at its brightest. Gentle winds whistled through the large Pindo palm trees that guarded our privacy.

'So how have you been?' I began. 'How was your visit to the Soaring Club? Did you get to fly?' I could see that Harry was struggling today. Maybe he had just taken his meds, or perhaps the reality was setting in that he was not long for this earth.

'Well, doc, what can I say?' Harry said, his voice weaker than before. 'I took my last flight in this world with Susan last weekend, and I also prepared my send-off flight to my next destination. As you see, I am hunched over, and I know it is due to cancer cells eating away at my bones. I used to wear suspenders for fashion and style in what seems to be another lifetime. Now I wear a back support out of necessity.

'On top of all that, you gave me a third limb of a cane just to walk. Reminds me of my days as a toddler. What an irony. I'm reliving my youth all over again, only I'm regressing physically and ageing mentally. I get it now. I get it.'

I was hesitant to respond, unsure if he was being sarcastic from frustration or if this was more of his usual jovial conversation.

'Come on, doc. Let's finish this race as quickly as possible before I lose my body. First, I want to hear about Eastern philosophies. Then tell me about your friend John. It looks like you were quite close to him.'

'Sure,' I replied. 'Let's start with my religion, Hinduism. Then we can look at Buddhism. However, I will keep my personal beliefs about death, life and the afterlife for our last discourse.'

'As long as you keep that promise and I am alive till then!' Harry reminded me.

Death in Hinduism is a family event. Most deaths occur at home. With mortality accepted as part of the normal human life cycle, a majority of Hindus accept life and death as destiny. Fatality and the finality of life are perceived as an illusion, called 'maya', a larger universal part of the plan of the Almighty.

Hindus perceive life as a journey to a much higher level of awareness. They seek liberation through multiple births and deaths. Human existence is perceived as a duality. The body is composed of five elements that constitute the corpus, with life force inserted by the Almighty. After death, the soul separates from the body. For thirteen days, it lingers around the family as they complete the post-death rituals. During these thirteen days, there are rituals, which include prayers offering 'Pitru Tarpan', a plea to the ancestors for the safe passage of the departed soul to rebirth. The family also prays for the rebirth of their loved one, so that, ultimately, the soul can achieve liberation.

Family, friends and priests all help the dying individual maintain as much mental equanimity as possible as death approaches. Therefore, family members and priests chant mantras, the names of deities and passages from texts that emphasize the immortality of the soul, in the presence of the dying loved one. A specific prayer, called 'Maha Mrutunjaya Jaap', addressed to Lord Shiva, is recited round the clock. This prayer emphasizes the immortality of the soul and asks for a peaceful, painless death. Translated, it says, 'We worship Lord Shiva, who enhances prosperity. May he liberate us from death like a ripe coconut separating effortlessly from its tree and not withhold its immortality.'

All the senses are engaged—including the sense of touch, by gently rubbing the body, the sense of hearing through chants, and the sense of smell through the aroma of incense. The family surrounds the dying individual, providing a comfortable transition from the physical body back to the immortal soul—either through reincarnation or spiritual accession, depending on how far the soul has developed. The goal of these processes is to move the consciousness of the individual from the human to the divine. Every act in Hindu tradition is considered a sacrifice, also called 'yagna'. The death rites are termed 'antyesthi', or the final sacrifice.

After death, Hindus generally do not embalm or attempt to preserve the body. The corpse is placed on the floor or the ground, where it is then purified and prepared for its journey. This involves bathing the body, pouring clarified butter into the mouth, wrapping the body in cloth, adorning it with flowers and anointing it with sandalwood paste. Males are taken for cremation as soon as possible. Females are taken for cremation the following day if the death has occurred in the late hours of the day.

The body is placed on a stretcher made of bamboo and ropes, covered in simple white cotton cloth, and carried on the shoulders of the family members to the cremation, often beside a river. The procession, which involves the chanting of mantras, is led by the eldest son, who takes the lead in all the funeral rites and rituals. He carries an earthen urn as well as a lit torch. Among Hindus, women do not go to the cremation site.

Close male relatives perform the cremation. In earlier days, they used to build the funeral pyre, but nowadays, electric crematoria are more common in metropolitan cities. Rural villages still build wooden pyres. The corpse is placed on the pyre, with the feet facing south, the direction from which 'Yama', the Hindu god of death, is said to arrive. The eldest son, with his head shaved and wearing white, walks around the body three times and then lights the fire at the corpse's feet. The soul is generally believed to exit the body from a point on the top of the head, called the 'brahmarandhra' or 'brahma gap', the place of the highest chakra. In some communities, this release is facilitated by cracking the skull open with a bamboo stick. This job also belongs to the eldest son.

After the cremation, mourners briefly bathe in the adjoining river to conclude the ritual. Bathing is a way to cleanse oneself of the impurity and danger associated with being in the presence of death. Upon the conclusion of the cremation, the ashes are collected in an urn and carried back by the eldest son. Then the thirteen days of rituals begin.

Among the tasks accomplished by cremation, and its preceding and succeeding rituals, are purification of the body, release of the soul from the body, and, if 'moksha' has not been attained, the creation of another body to provide for the passage into the next realm and, ultimately, rebirth.

Deeply pious believers with the means to afford it sometimes choose to die in Benares, or Varanasi, considered the holiest city in Hinduism, on the banks of the holy river Ganga. They go to Varanasi to die, be cremated and have their ashes poured into the river, as it is believed that death in Varanasi liberates the deceased from the cycle of life and death. Dying in this city is thought to enable a person to escape rebirth and achieve liberation, or moksha.

Children who die under the age of five, along with people considered to have achieved sainthood, are not cremated but buried. It is believed that their souls are pure and do not need the purifying rituals of cremation. Some are buried sitting up in the lotus posture.

Hindus believe that after undergoing rebirth through multiple species (8.4 million life forms), an individual finally achieves the much-coveted birth as a human being. This is the only form of life in which an individual can complete the cycles of birth and death, and achieve ultimate liberation or salvation, or 'moksha' in Sanskrit (also known as 'nirvana' in Buddhism).

But the thought of being born again and again does not provide comfort to Hindus. It just means that all of life's suffering will be experienced repeatedly. This suffering results from our attachment to impermanent things. The process of rebirth is driven by the production of 'karma'. Karma is like a moral law of cause and effect. While good karma leads to more desirable rebirths, bad karma can land one in misery. The goal is to cease production of karma altogether so as not to fuel the cycle for another round of rebirth.

Beliefs about the nature of liberation, however, differ among Hindus. If one believes in a non-dualistic conception of reality, where 'atman' and 'Brahman' are the same, then liberation means recognizing this identity, thus ending the cycle of rebirth.

Some Hindus, however, are dualists who believe that atman and Brahman are separate. For them, liberation is abiding forever in the presence of the divine, ultimate reality: Brahman.

Harry was obviously tired from following everything I said. Unlike some of our previous meetings, he simply listened without asking many questions. I knew that hearing about the Hindu belief system, in a nutshell, had likely been a tough challenge for him.

'Okay,' he said, taking a long breath. 'That's a lot to process, but I appreciate the overview. How about Islam? Have you studied Islamic death rituals?'

Apparently, Harry had the strength to proceed.

'Harry, I am neither a religious scholar, nor do I claim to be an authority. However, I have had a good number of friends who have been Muslims, and I can share what I vaguely remember. I may have to ask for forgiveness if my memory is not accurate.'

Harry said, 'Well, if we can keep it brief, I think I'm up for a summary. I really do value this survey you're providing . . .' He paused to swallow and take another breath. '. . . Because it's helping me fine-tune my own beliefs before I die.'

In Islam, sharia typically calls for the burial of the body as soon as possible, preceded by a simple ritual involving bathing and shrouding the body, followed by 'salah', or Islamic prayer.

Burial is usually within twenty-four hours of death to protect the living from sanitary issues. They allow exceptions— for example, if many people are killed in battle and if foul play is suspected and needs to be investigated. In those cases, it is important to determine the cause of death before burial. Islam prohibits cremation of the body, as it amounts to desecration of it.

In Islam, the corpse is bathed in hot water. This should be done as soon as possible after death, preferably within hours. It is commonly done by same-gender adult members of the immediate family. The corpse is typically wrapped in a simple plain cloth known as the *kafan*. This is done to respect the dignity and privacy of the deceased. The kafan is simple and modest. It is for this reason that Muslims generally prefer to use a white cotton cloth as a shroud. The deceased may be kept in this state for several hours, allowing well-wishers to pass on their respects and condolences. Muslims of the community gather to offer their collective prayers for the forgiveness of the sins of the dead.

The lowering of the corpse and positioning of the soil is done by the next of kin. In the case of a deceased husband, a brother or a brother-in-law usually performs this task. In the case of a deceased wife, the husband undertakes this if physically able to; otherwise, the eldest son or the son-in-law is responsible for lowering, aligning and propping up the deceased. Those present symbolically pour three handfuls of soil into the grave while reciting a Quranic verse that translates to: 'We created you from it, and return you into it, and from it, we will raise you a second time.' More prayers are then said, further asking for forgiveness of the deceased and reminding the dead of their profession of faith.

The corpse is then fully buried by the gravediggers, who may stamp or pat down the grave. Grief at the death of a beloved person and weeping for the dead is normal and acceptable.

'So,' Harry said, 'the death and burial customs among Muslims are not too different from those of other Abrahamic faiths, right?'

'You could say that,' I agreed, 'but keep in mind that Islamic beliefs about God, life and the afterlife differ substantially from Christianity and Judaism. While death and burial rituals may be similar in some ways, I wouldn't want you to confuse the general beliefs of the three Abrahamic religions. They have common roots in Abraham, but they are very different in theology and doctrine.

'We're touching only upon the beliefs and processes of death and the afterlife,' I continued, clarifying. 'This isn't a course in comparative religions, my friend. We're not covering everything, or even the essential tenets, of each belief system.'

'I understand, doc.' Harry was tracking with me. Then he asked, 'What about Buddhists? Are they similar to your faith in Hinduism?'

According to Buddhism, the aim at the time of death is this: Don't think about some possible afterlife, don't worry about what will happen to others after you die, and don't go back on how you lived your life. Just directly attend to the dying process. Become mindful of the process of dying.

In Buddhism, once death occurs, the deceased may be cremated or buried. Cremation is more common than burial. Buddhist monks, if available, will perform last rites before the casket is sealed. Family members may assist in lifting the casket as a final act of service, while others attending may observe a moment of respectful silence. During the funeral procession, family members walk behind the hearse. At a traditional Buddhist funeral, the family wears white or covers their clothing with a traditional white cloth, along with a headband or an armband. Mourners may also chant or sing appropriate sutras, or prayers, bring offerings of flowers and fruit, burn incense to sweeten the air or ring gongs or bells.

Death is not seen as an end in Buddhism. It is perceived as only a transition from one form to another. The focus during post-death rituals is on understanding the transience of life, thinking about one's own mortality as an impetus to making life meaningful, and performing good deeds on behalf of the deceased person. Like Hindus, Buddhists believe in samsara—the cycle of death and rebirth—and that samsara is driven by karma.

Buddhists generally believe that there are six possible realms of rebirth. One of these is the human realm. Above the human realm are two other realms. The lower of these is the realm of beings called 'asuras', also perceived as demi-gods or titans. Their lives are certainly not peaceful. At the highest realm are the devas, the deities who live blissfully. Just below humans is the realm of the animals. Below them is the realm of the hungry ghosts, who are perpetually unsatisfied. At the lowest level is the realm of hell.

While some Buddhists see these realms as actual places, others see them more metaphorically. In the course of a single day, we can move from a heavenly realm as we eat a delicious meal or get some great news, to a hellish realm as some tragedy befalls us. In other words, rebirth is ongoing—all the time. One way to think of our lives is as continuity without identity. There is a chain of continuity—a karmic chain of causes and conditions—that leads from the infant, to the adolescent, to the adult. When a person dies, the karmic inheritance from his or her life gives rise to a new being. But through it all, there is no unchanging, enduring element.

All these realms are temporary. The ultimate goal is to get off the cycle of all these realms, liberate oneself from samsara and attain nirvana.

The Buddha was originally a Hindu named Gautama by birth. He saw suffering, old age and death, and received no satisfactory answer for why they occurred—hindering his own quest for inner peace. He then began his search for eternal truth and answers to all of his spiritual questions. Once he became the Buddha, the Enlightened One, he used plain and simple language to share his learnings.

He framed his teachings in a detailed account of mindfulness meditation. The basic approach is to sit in a stable posture and observe the movement of your breath as it comes into and goes out of your body. As you try to keep your attention on the breath, a flood of thoughts, memories, plans and anxieties will demand and often make your attention waver. With a great deal of practice, however, you will learn to observe all of these things without clinging to them, and return your attention to your breathing.

Why does mindfulness meditation work? First, it shows us that most, if not all, of our suffering is self-inflicted. The regrets over past mistakes, the fears about the future, the anger and frustration over our failures, and so many other painful aspects of our lives are produced by the mind. If the mind can be transformed, the suffering will end. Bringing the mind back to the present moment, the experience of the body and breath, and being able to observe from the stable platform of centred awareness, diminishes the power of negative thoughts and emotions.

The Buddha said, 'While we can aim to make things better, of course, we must start from the recognition of reality, an acceptance of the way things are.'

I noticed what looked like a grimace of pain on Harry's face. 'How are you doing, my friend?' I asked.

'Hurting a bit,' Harry said. 'And tired. You've given me lots to think about. Can we stop today, but meet again tomorrow? I know my time is getter shorter. But I do want to hear about John.'

He gingerly adjusted his posture.

'For you, Harry, I will be happy to adjust my schedule tomorrow. And I'll tell you about John. I think you'll get a lot out of his story.'

We set a time for the next day and said goodbye. Each time I bid farewell to Harry, I wondered if it would be for the last time.

10

John's Goodbye

Life is like a journey on a train ... with its stations with changes
or routes and tracks.

We board this train when we are born, and our parents are the
ones who get us this ticket.

We believe they will always travel with us on this train.
However, at some stations, our parents will get off the train
one at a time, leaving us alone on this journey.

Sometimes they stay on, and we get off the train earlier, leaving
them to grieve for us.

As time goes by, other passengers board the train. They are our
siblings, friends or our spouses and loved ones.

Many will get off the journey and leave a permanent vacuum
in our lives.

Many will go unnoticed that we won't even know when they
vacated their seats and got off the train!

This train ride will be full of joy, sorrow, fantasy, expectations,
hellos and goodbyes.

A good journey is helping, loving, having good relationships
with all co-passengers and making sure we give our best to
make their journey comfortable.

The mystery of this fabulous journey is: We do not know we ourselves are getting off.

So, we must live in the best way—adjust, forget, forgive and offer the best of what we have.

—Author unknown

'Hi, Kashyap, this is John.'

I was taken aback. John never called me at home or on weekends. My wife and I were getting ready to go see my son Maharshi at Duke University and take him out to dinner. The only time John had called during non-business hours was when his mother, Lily, was dying. Before I could solve the puzzle of his unusual timing, I remembered that I had promised John I would help him celebrate his fifth year of remission from cancer.

'Hey, John! So good to hear from you. What's up?' I was somewhat apologetic as I had been meaning to call him. 'I was planning a big party for your victory over your cancer. You chased it away! Let me know some dates, and I'll start getting things together.'

There was awkward silence at the other end.

'Are you okay? Is everyone all right in your family? I still recall the funny conversations we had at Maharshi's send-off to join the Blue Devils at Duke. We had a great time.'

'I'm afraid it's over, Kashyap,' John said sombrely.

'What do you mean?'

'Kashyap, it's all over,' John said again. 'The beast came back with a vengeance a month after we dropped Maharshi off at Duke.'

I could feel my heart pounding at his news. 'Tell me what happened. I know there are many options out there. Latest therapies, new surgical procedures—we can try many things . . .'

'Sorry to interrupt, but I did some of those promising options, and they did not work. I have, maybe, a few weeks. If I'm lucky, a couple of months. So my docs say. They want to keep trying too. But I feel like I'm done with it all. Time for me to move on.'

John sounded resigned to the inevitable. 'I wanted to call you and let you know I have decided to pack my bags and move on, literally and figuratively, away from Charlotte and beyond this human life. Do you remember my beach house at Ocean Isle, where we sailed and had lots of fun with jet skis?'

'Yes, yes, I loved that place. I would love to retire to a place like that.' My desire now was to cut short the painful parts of the discussion and keep John focused on happier times.

'Well,' John continued, 'I'm going to retire from work and life to move down there to prepare for my journey beyond this life. I've packed my bags. I've given away whatever I could, while holding on to a few sweet and sour memories. I wish I could erase all memories and press Ctrl+Alt+Del to reboot the bad memories and enjoy the rest of the days. Never mind. We have to go through our destiny.'

'You sound like a philosopher, my friend! I never knew you were so good at such metaphors!'

'I was and I wasn't. Time changes everything, Kashyap. I hope you'll never have to go through what I have been through in my life. I lost everything. My battle against cancer, my sanity, my house and my sweet wife.' John paused briefly. 'Now I am patiently awaiting the Grim Reaper's arrival for me.'

Understandably, he sounded discouraged and sad. I had no words to console him, no strength to infuse any optimism into him, no language to ease his anguish. Finally, I gathered the courage and asked, 'Where are you, John? Can I come and see you right now?'

'Well, I'm moving down to the beach today. Lots to catch up on. I wish I had the time to catch up with you and put some closure to our lives together.'

As John was speaking, Robert Frost's words were ringing in my ears:

The woods are lovely, dark and deep
And I have promises to keep
And miles to go before I sleep
And miles to go before I sleep.

'Listen, Kashyap, I wanted to say goodbye, forever, for sure.' His voice sounded choked. 'Please convey my love to Alpa, Maharshi, TJ, Bobby, Charles and Jim.'

'John, I will visit you at the beach as soon as I can.'

'I may not be alive then. See if you can. If not, I sure will wait for you in unknown lands, maybe in heaven. Goodbye for now.'

John hung up.

Later in the week, I called up Charles, our mutual friend who had been close to both of us. I explained the situation. He was as sad to hear the news as I had been.

'What do you want to do?' Charles asked. 'It looks like you miss seeing him. Do you want to drive down there? I could come with you. I need to do some work at my beach house there. I will gladly join you, see John, then finish my work and drive back.'

'Let's go tomorrow,' I said. 'Let me confirm with his sister, Nancy, that he can see us.'

Nancy was with John at his beach house and greeted me warmly on the phone. 'Doug and I were just talking about you. I'm glad you called . . . John keeps talking about your visit to our mother when she left this world.'

'I was planning to drive down there to check on him,' I said.

'Just the thing we were waiting to hear. I hate to make you drive such a long distance, but we sure will appreciate it if you can make it.'

'On my way, Nan.'

Charles was kind enough to drive as we left early the next morning. The sky was overcast and the sun hid behind a gloomy winter sky. The five-hour journey felt like five days. John had not only been my patient's son. As an attorney, he had helped me personally when my career was going through a dark patch. He was the light that had drawn me out of hopelessness and despair. He inspired me to keep doing what I could in my professional career, being a guardian angel. Since I had lost my brother to a traumatic death in India, John had served as my mentor, guide and protector. Today, I was going to see him, perhaps for the last time, to bid him goodbye.

The sky was still overcast, and the ocean behind John's home roiled, compounding the sense of impending gloom. I rang the doorbell just once, almost hesitating to intrude. Nancy came to the door, hugged Charles and me, and cried as she brought us up to date.

Then she led us to John's bedroom. This was his favourite room, overlooking the Atlantic Ocean. We stood silent for a few minutes and watched as John was under the effect of morphine to mitigate his pain. Charles left the room as I sat on the chair at John's bedside.

I could not believe the sight of his face and body. He snored under the heavy sedation of morphine, and his mouth gasped for air between deep, scattered breaths. His face had no fat or feature, literally just skin and bones. His eyes would open and close only to reveal dry, sunken eyes that seemed to search for something or someone. His neck muscles looked like little shrivelled threads connecting the loose bones of his collar and jaw.

I took John's hand in mine and whispered, 'How are you, John? It's Kashyap. I'm here. I hope you are doing okay.'

Like an early slow-motion movie, John opened his eyes, rolled his eyes around, and spoke. 'So, you did make it here on time, Kashyap. My mind was not convinced you would make it, but my heart said you would. You are not too late. I am still sane, in between my naps, and I can think and speak.'

'Are you in pain, John? How are you coping?'

He swallowed hard. 'To be honest, all my pain and suffering has gone . . . and I am at complete peace with myself and the world. The last time we talked, I was struggling to accept my defeat. As a litigator, I always wanted to win. I used to always see life in black and white . . . with no grey in between. Now that I have accepted my existence in the grey zone, I am at peace with everything.

'Look, you are here, my entire family is here. Even my ex-wife is here. What can be better? You know, Kashyap, life is . . . about living in balance and compromise. It is . . . oops. Can you push that pump for me? I got overexcited and hurt myself. I need an extra dose of morphine.'

'Here you go.' I administered an extra dose of morphine to ease his discomfort.

'Thank you,' John said as his body relaxed slightly. 'Remember those days back in 2003 and 2004, when we met regularly and talked about shaping up your practice?'

'I do, John. How can I forget the most important chapter in my life that defines me today? I remember long evenings and weekends together. I owe my existence here today to you and your mentorship and guidance. I would not be here if not for you.'

'You know the one thing that matters most?'

'Tell me, John.' My friend was acting as my big brother again.

'That nothing matters in the end except your devotion to the cause you serve. If you feel that you have . . . fulfilled your mission to the best of your abilities, everything else—money, materialistic things, and everything else—is irrelevant. I'm glad I learnt it . . . though it took cancer for me to get the message. In the end, nothing matters except your honesty, integrity and unwavering dedication to your calling.'

He paused to rest and catch his breath, then fell asleep again.

I sat there quietly, observing his dissolving body—what a change. Just six months ago, John was healthy and hearty; now, he was dissolving right before my eyes. I gently rubbed his forearms. He woke up again, his eyelids hanging like a shell covering delicate marine life. His eyes were sunken, with dry crust around the corners of the eyes. Opening an eyelid was like lifting heavy weights for him. But he did not give up.

'Kashyap, look at my forearm. Can you see my wrist bones? What do you call them in your medical language?' He pointed to the meatless bones. A cannula had been inserted in the vein of his left forearm for a continuous supply of morphine. Another cannula was attached to the main tributary to allow booster shots if the pain became too much. As each drop of liquid morphine dripped into his veins, it created a small blob that gently dissolved and disappeared further downstream. Another large cannula was hanging from the side of John's blanket, allowing him to urinate without having to get up.

'Yes, John, I can see that,' I said. 'We call these bones the ulna and the radius.'

He then pointed to the open windows on both sides of his bedroom. John's beach house was in a great location on Ocean Isle Beach—a pearl situated at the junction of intercoastal waterways to the west and the Atlantic Ocean to the east. From there, you could see the complete arc of the sun's orbit from sunrise to sunset.

Nancy had opened all the windows. To my surprise, the clouds had lifted and the midday sun was shining at full intensity, though on its way to the west now.

'You see, Kashyap . . . that powerful glory of the almighty sun? Do you see that blinding reflection . . . from the rising and falling waves?'

'Yes, I do,' I replied. 'It's so bright that I can't even look at it. If I continue to stare, I might go blind.'

'This is the story of my life, and that of everyone,' John went on. 'Every morning through evening, I see myself born like a crisp dawn, rising to the fullest glory . . . and dying every evening, to be reborn again the next morning. I have lost count of the number of days that I see the repetition of my life. Morning reminds me of my childhood days of innocence . . . playing around in the gentle, cool breeze as the soothing rays of the rising sun brings warmth and comfort.'

He paused and then pointed to his glass of water. I brought it to him. He took a sip but was suddenly racked by a violent cough, almost spilling the water.

But he managed to continue. 'The midday sun is almost like the height of glory in my career . . . when I was lead attorney in the mergers of the largest financial institutions in the late 1990s. I did not cast a shadow and there was no doubt or darkness to my success. Everything was so bright . . .'

He paused again and pointed for a booster dose of morphine. I respected his desire. 'And now, I am like that setting sun, slowly losing its brightness, shine, warmth and glory, waiting to sink into the horizon . . . except that I may not emerge again the next morning.'

He exhaled and closed his eyes again. I sensed that there was still something he wanted to share, perhaps his last message.

I stayed in the chair beside him.

The evening sun had drifted towards the intercoastal waterways. It was steadily losing its glory and lustre, almost as if it had been subdued. The waters were now pale yellow, and the western sky was turning crimson red.

John opened his eyes again. 'Kashyap, listen, my brother. I have always felt a deep sense of connection with you . . . and your family. Please convey my love to Alpa and Maharshi. I thank you for being part of our lives . . . for the last several years.'

Slowly, John turned his gaze towards the ocean. He tried to lift his left hand, but to no avail. He may have been trying to point to the sunset in relation to his own life's sunset. His eyes closed. His breathing became shallower and more laboured. Death rattles from his mouth disrupted the pin-drop silence.

I rose, walked into the hallway and called for the family to come. Nancy and Doug, my friend Charles, and John's ex-wife, Paula, joined me, and we gathered around his bed. Nancy held his hands with tears running down her cheeks.

I said softly, 'John, we are all here with you. I know you can hear us, and you can feel our loving touch. You have been a wonderful brother, father, husband, son and friend. It breaks my heart to utter these words, but you have our permission to go. We will miss you, but it's time to move on. Your mother, Lily, is waiting for you in heaven. Please leave whenever you are ready.'

His eyes rolled open for a brief moment. He gazed at the ocean. The evening sun had lost its glow and was nearly touching the water on the western horizon. John closed his eyes, never to open them again on this earth.

* * *

John's story had moved Harry. And he could see the pain in my face as I spoke about losing my dearest friend. John's story showed him that cancer never discriminated between the haves and have-nots. John had been successful beyond what most people could have ever dreamt of. He had money, and he had power, but that did little to comfort him in the end. Finally, it was just the peace of a beautiful sunset on the ocean waters that eased his passage to eternity.

'Oh my . . .' Harry exhaled, before being interrupted by a cough.

'Are you okay? Do you need water?' I asked.

'No, thanks . . .' He took a deep breath before he could speak. 'Doc, sometimes, I can see myself sinking and drowning.

At times . . . I feel I just want to drown deep into an ocean, never to rise again.' He needed to catch a few breaths before he could complete his sentences.

Then he asked, 'Do you always get attached to your patients? How can you continue to do so all the time? Don't you ever get burnt out . . . from doing this over and over again?'

'Not really, Harry. I get a sense of fulfilment from helping my fellow human beings.'

'Okay, then tell me if you see any value or reason for this life . . . and death. Do you ever envision immortality . . . being achievable? Is it possible?'

'I will share what science and society see as the value of death. Then I will share where I stand.'

'I know I am taking a lot of your valuable time . . . but do you think we can address that tomorrow?'

'Of course,' I said.

He had begun counting the days.

11

The Quest for Immortality

You are neither earth, nor water, nor fire, nor wind or space
For the sake of freedom, know yourself as the embodiment of
pure eternal consciousness and witness thereof
You are unbound pure awareness, supreme eternal bliss, in
which universe appears like the mirage of a snake in a rope.
Be happy.

—Ashtavakra

Since the beginning of time, human beings have been on a quest
to defy death. Records show the quest for immortality dating as
far back as the first emperor of China, Qin Shihuang. He was
obsessed with attaining immortality. He sent expeditions to
find the secret to it, rumoured to be on the mythical island of
Penglai, home to immortals. When this island was never located,
he instructed his court chemists to formulate a compound that
would give him immortality. His court alchemists concocted an
elixir with mercury at its base. As you can imagine, drinking this
elixir eventually killed him.

Many pursued the secret of immortality in other parts of the world. Alchemy was practised regularly during the medieval period in the Middle East among Islamic communities, and in Europe in many religions, as well as by non-religious leaders and cultures. Muslims of the great Islamic Umayyad and Abbasid caliphates developed empirical approaches to it, which served as precursors to the more well-known European alchemy of the early twelfth century.

Later, in the seventeenth and eighteenth centuries, Sir Isaac Newton devoted significant time to alchemical studies, believing he could eventually discover the philosopher's stone, which is thought to grant immortal life. With the medical advancements the scientific revolution brought, however, alchemy fell into disfavour.

'Harry,' I said as he visited the following morning, 'imagine that only you were granted immortality. What would it be like to see everyone you have ever loved—your friends, your children—all die one by one around you as you continue to linger on for centuries? What would that kind of life look like?'

'Not good, doc. When everyone that I knew died, what would be the point of living?'

'Indeed, Harry. I agree with you! Yet, there are other ways to look at it. Depending on one's religious leaning, there is the possibility of personal immortality in several theological or metaphysical modes—from physical resurrection and spiritual survival as a disembodied soul to reincarnation. The other possibility is through familial immortality. Our genes are passed down to our children, and to their children after them. Thus, our DNA continues to be part of the fabric of this world, even after we're gone.

'We can also leave behind a legacy through the influence we have on others. This form of immortality exists in the impact we have on individual lives—family, friends, students and members of our community. Even after we are gone, that influence remains, to be passed on to their children and their children's children.

'And when we die, we release back to the earth the elements we borrowed from it that constituted our body. These elements eventually give birth to new life forms and organisms. The elements of our body participate in the natural world long after we are gone. You can take comfort in the fact that your death will be part of the cyclical process of nature.'

'Like when my friend drops my ashes over where I used to fly?'

'Just like that, my friend. That one act alone will make you immortal. But I want you to remember all the good you've done for those around you . . . for society, in general. The love and life you've given Susan and your children. The good you've accomplished through your work. The friends you've loved and encouraged. Yours is a legacy any man would be proud of. Regardless of your spiritual beliefs, all of those things make you immortal!'

Harry shifted in his chair, paused a moment, then shifted back. As he adjusted himself again, he said, 'You've told me about what your religion believes and what different people believe. What about you, personally?'

'Well, Harry, I see my own immortality through oneness—or non-duality—with all existence. This was an idea expressed in the ancient philosophical Upanishads, and rehearsed by Ashtavakra and Sankaracharya, two of my favourite Indian philosophers. Such a state is described in almost every religious tradition and can be realized through meditation.'

'So, you think that immortality is really something that humanity can achieve in different ways . . . without existing in this body. But since we're just here for a short time and then die . . . what does it all mean?'

'Harry, despite all of the psychological, existential and philosophical challenges death confronts us with, I believe that death is what makes a meaningful life possible, knowing what little time we have makes every day precious, and each moment sacred. Recognizing that we can pass on something enduring from ourselves to those who will follow us can give us a powerful sense of purpose, even if the brevity of our existence tinges our days with wistfulness.'

Harry said nothing. But I could see in his eyes the kind of wistfulness I had just mentioned.

I continued, 'If death is the end of us, does it make life meaningless? Or is it what makes life meaningful? Death is paradoxical in many ways. Death is bad, yet not bad for the person who dies. It is both important to hold on to it, and essential to let go of it. We are justified in fearing death, and yet we should recognize that death is what gives our life meaning.

'Harry, death is one of our most powerful teachers. Hopefully, the wisdom we gain from reflecting on the impermanence of all around us, and from exploring the ideas of those who have faced and thought deeply about death and loss, will help us die better when the time comes—and to live wiser, richer and more fulfilling lives while we have them. Just as you're doing, Harry.'

'Just as you're helping me do, doc,' my friend said.

12

The Fourth Dimension

Never was there a time that I did not exist, nor you, or these kings,
Nor will there be a time when we cease to be.
Just as this body goes through the cycles of childhood, youth and old age,
So after death, it passes to another body.
Just as you discard old worn-out clothes, and put on new ones,
The Self discards old worn-out bodies and takes on a new one.
These bodies come to an end; but the vast embodied Self is eternal, ageless and fathomless.
Death is certain for this body and rebirth is certain for the deceased.
Why do you grieve, then?
The Self was never born. It is birthless and primordial. It never dies.
Knowing that the Self is eternal, indestructible and unborn, how could it ever perish?
The Self can't be pierced or singed, moistened or withered. It is vast, all-pervading, eternal, serene and timeless.

—Bhagavad Gita

'Well,' Harry said as we found our seats the next day, 'I think this beast has taken over my body . . . my fibre, my bones and my muscles . . . one at a time.'

He was breathing heavily from our short walk to the garden dome.

'I can see the bright light at the end of the tunnel,' he continued after a few moments. 'Physically, I am weaker . . . maybe close to broken. But emotionally, I am calmer. I . . . have become familiar with the dissolution of my physical body . . . and have arranged for Susan and my daughters to take care of my mortal remains.

'However, I am still somewhat confused about the afterlife . . . and the journey to the . . . destination unknown. Doc, would you now show me your cards? What is your learning leading to? Where do you think you will head . . . after your own journey?'

Harry paused to catch his breath. 'Looks like my time is very limited now. I think this may be . . . the last time I visit you.'

I wanted to be honest but encouraging. 'Harry, while I see your physical body is degenerating, your indestructible self is slowly rising to the level of awareness that will help you prepare for the ultimate journey. My favourite author, Richard Bach, wrote this: "The mark of your ignorance is the depth of your belief in injustice and tragedy. What the caterpillar calls the end of the world, the Master calls a butterfly."'

Harry appeared bewildered. 'What is death, then? Are you saying that you think there is no injustice or tragedy in death?'

'Not at all, friend. I don't intend to convey that I lack empathy. However, when I trace my own journey of learning, and my own understanding, after the moment of pain and sense of loss that comes with death, I rise to get a bird's-eye view, to see the panorama, not just the microcosm. My response changes from sadness to acceptance—and also to a better understanding of life across all levels of existence.'

'Still not quite getting it . . .' Harry said.

I tried a different tack. 'Harry, have you ever been to Africa, in the wilderness?'

'Yes. As an RAF pilot, I've been on trips to Tanzania and Kenya. But how does it relate to what we are talking about?'

'Have you seen the great migration of wildebeest across the crocodile-infested Grumeti and the Mara rivers? It is an amazing yet awful sight. Thousands of wildebeest run across a river infested with crocodiles during the migration season, and many are killed during the crossing. Despite the horror, it is one of the most spectacular sights in Africa. And if you happen to be lucky, you may even witness a buffalo being hunting by multiple lionesses!'

'I have seen both,' Harry said. 'It is hard to forget those sights.'

'Good. You are helping me make my point. So what amounted to a memorable incident from your perspective would have been totally different for the buffalo trying to cross the river. What you saw as a thrilling sight of a hunted buffalo may have led to orphaned calves! Did you ever think of their reaction? What you see as a most memorable river crossing, where hundreds of wildebeest become food for crocodiles in the Grumeti, is entirely different for their offspring, now motherless.'

I paused briefly to help Harry see my perspective.

'I get it, doc. So what was an entertaining view of nature for me was a tragedy for another. But these are not human beings. They are animals! Wouldn't you react differently if it was a human and not an animal? Hunting is part of what nature intended for them.'

'Well, I do not want to sound contrarian, but cats and dogs are also animals. You have a cat yourself, don't you?'

'Yes! More than one, in fact.'

'Are they not animals too?'

'Of course . . .'

'So how do you differentiate one animal life from another? Simply because deer, buffalo and wildebeest are born in the jungles of Africa does not diminish the value of their life compared to domesticated pets.'

'I see your point,' my friend nodded. 'But then, how will wild predators survive?'

'I am glad that you are reaching an understanding of life that I have reached too. For herbivorous animals inhabiting the savannahs in Africa, life is always in peril, and when we look at the food chain and predator ecology, one comes to an acceptance of the circle of life.

'It's all about perspective. From the point of view of a lion, life is all about hunting prey. It may sound like a violent life, but when you take a bird's-eye view, you understand—and accept— the right of a predator to attack and prey on other animals further down the food chain. So what may look like tragedy for one is really the survival for another species.'

I proceeded, 'When we look at the caterpillar evolving into a butterfly, there is transformation from one life form to another— from crawling on tiny legs to flitting freely from flower to flower. Its life ceases as a caterpillar and begins as a butterfly.

'For my learning, Harry, I have come to realize that we can slowly rise above the ideas of mortality and finitude of life. I've found that if we take a reductionist approach and analyse each event in isolation, rejoicing or regretting individual happenings, life appears full of paradoxes and contradiction. However, when we take a higher panoramic view, combining every moment we have lived, we develop a completely different perspective.'

Harry was silent, contemplative.

'For example,' I went on, 'when you start learning how to play the piano, separated notes sound harsh and occasionally disruptive. However, when you combine them in the right sequence, you instead hear a magical symphony. So, when you move from the microcosm to the macrocosm, you may be able to rise above the finitude and finality of human life and death. When you look above and beyond the confines of space and time, you may fully understand the continuum of all forms of life, inseparable from each other. Death, then, may sound like a temporary pause in the eternity of existence.'

'But how do you develop that higher perspective?'

'Harry, just as you fly to develop a bird's-eye view, you may also develop your understanding of life beyond the five senses. You may expand your comprehension of life beyond what you can see, feel, touch, hear and smell.'

'But my world exists within the confines of my senses,' Harry pushed back. 'My senses allow me to interact with the outside world. Are there things beyond what my senses can experience?'

'Really, Harry, do you think you can see everything? Even microscopic? Until Antonie van Leeuwenhoek invented the microscope, humanity's vision was limited by what it could see unaided. Then the microscope enabled us to see life beyond that. Similarly, Hans Lippershey developed the first telescope. As a result, we can explore the mysteries of deep space. Now, we are able to see things at the microscopic level and far into deep space, altering beliefs held for several millennia.'

Harry nodded, granting the point. 'Okay. What does this have to do with death and dying?'

'I am trying to connect the dots, my friend. As I was saying when I mentioned the chords of music, we can understand the grand scale of life and death better as we learn to view something in its entire context rather than merely its individual components. Doing so enables us to start comprehending the fourth dimension of existence.'

Harry held up a hand, as though asking me to pause a moment. 'The fourth dimension, doc? There's height, width and depth . . . I'm not thinking of a fourth one.'

I smiled to acknowledge his question. 'What I mean by the fourth dimension is life or energy within a physical form that persists and remains in existence. By a purely physical or philosophical definition, an entity or object's persistence through eternal time is like its extension through space. Thus, an object that exists in time has temporal parts in the various sub-regions of the total region of time it occupies, just like an object that exists in a region of space has at least one part in every sub-region of that space. I realize that's a mouthful to comprehend.'

'I'll say,' Harry smiled back.

Not wanting to lose the train of thought, I went on. 'According to supporters of the fourth dimension of existence, time is analogous to space. Thus, the continuity of time and space leads to the possibility or probability of infinitesimal existence. For my understanding and approach to life and death, the fourth dimension is equivalent to an indestructible soul. This is a philosophical approach to the ontological nature of time, according to which all points in time are equally "real", as opposed to the idea that only the present is real. And just as all spatially distant objects and events are equally as real as those close to us, temporally distant objects and events are as real as those currently present to us.

'The inventions of the microscope and telescope have enabled us to define the three-dimensional structure of all matter, from small atoms to the infinite universe. When another scientist in the future develops a tool that transcends time, we will be able to comprehend the idea of the eternity of existence—of individual life merging into omniscient life as a time and space continuum.'

'I think I'm following you . . . well, mostly . . . I think,' Harry said, an embarrassed grin on his lips.

I knew I was dumping a truckload on him.

'Using your visual sense in an "infinite, expansive" fashion, open your vision beyond confinement to this physical body . . . and try and accept the indestructible nature of the core of your inner existence—this is your fourth dimension. While telescopes and microscopes are mechanical tools, when you dive into your microcosm, it will help you see yourself as a walking micro-ecosystem with trillions of miniature life forms and existences living in perfect harmony or symbiosis.'

'Wow. It sounds like we are a walking micro-planet. How do these many lives live with each other? How do they communicate?'

'This is precisely what I am trying to throw light on. Every day millions of cells are born in the human body, and millions of cells die. Some cells, like our neutrophils or white blood cells, live two–five days. Others live four–six months, and cells like our brain cells and lymphocytes live indefinitely. Those cells communicate with each other with wireless channels called cell signalling pathways. We witness the death and reincarnation of cells within our own body every single second. In fact, the latest research tells us that only 10 per cent of cells in our physical bodies are part of our tissue. The other cells are all microbes that use the body as a vehicle to propagate their own survival and existence for whatever little time they have. There is a whole world that exists within us.'

'Like Star Wars within our own bodies,' Harry chimed in. Then he shifted the topic a bit. 'Do you know if there is a way knowledge and information can traverse through generations? Is there a way the deceased can communicate with their protégés?'

'Harry, you are posing the right kind of questions.' I paused briefly and spotted a beautiful monarch butterfly settling on a beautiful Mexican petunia flower. 'Look at this beautiful butterfly.'

'Hey,' Harry said to the butterfly, 'we were just talking about you! Thanks for visiting us!'

'Perfect timing,' I agreed, 'because monarch butterflies are an answer to your question about transgenerational communication. They begin their life in Alaska. Towards early fall, they start their journey in mass flocks on a designated route. They fly over rivers, mountains, jungles and across national boundaries, through Canada to the US, and eventually to Mexico. They reach a specific forest in Mexico, where they hatch their eggs. They die after this and their protégés resume the journey, following the same route back to spend spring and summer in the same part of Alaska where they began their journey.'

Harry's eyes widened. 'I had no idea that these beautiful creatures would not only help me understand metamorphoses from caterpillars to butterflies, but also how life-sustaining information can be transferred through generations without a direct link. Your theory of soul and body makes sense, doc.'

I gave my friend a cursory visual examination. 'How are you doing, Harry? Is all this philosophical talk wearing you out?'

'So far, so good,' Harry replied. 'I told you I badly wanted to hear where your journey has brought you, and I'm determined to hear it. Like I said, who knows how much time I have or whether we'll be able to talk again.'

'All right,' I said gently. 'I'll continue, but stop me if you get too tired, okay?'

'Deal.'

'Harry, once you open yourself up to schools of higher learning, you will find that everything around us teaches new and unique lessons. When you look at herds of elephants in Africa and the way they communicate with each other, you will be amazed at their social life—often more organized than our own!'

'Explain, please.'

'Well, elephant herds communicate with each other across tens of miles by producing infrasound. These sounds are outside the audible range of most animals, including human beings. Zoologists have deciphered hundreds of different elephant signals that communicate the location of water, danger, even forest fires. When the massive Indian Ocean tsunami struck, elephants in zoos sensed it before any warning signals were picked up by technology. They broke their chains and tried to climb to higher points in their enclosures.

'In the event that an elephant dies, others can sense it miles away. They assemble, mourn and even bury their deceased. They periodically return to the burial site, shed tears and express grief.'

'Amazing,' Harry sighed. 'How do you learn all this, doc? You seem to have a very eclectic but real perspective on life and learning.'

'Harry, we are lifelong learners, observers and discoverers. Formal schools do not teach everything. Humans have been enquirers from the beginning of time. From scientists to mariners, curiosity has driven the discoverer and explorer to carry out lifelong journeys of learning. Some have even crossed normal or accepted boundaries of enquiry to the point where others have questioned their sanity.

'One big difference between Eastern and Western learners and enquirers is that the West has seemed to emphasize learning, enquiry and discovery outside the physical body. Albert Einstein, Sir Isaac Newton and their contemporaries are examples of individuals who went outside the body to learn and chase physics. Ancient Greek and Roman philosophers went the path of logical reasoning and conclusions.

'Contrary to that, Eastern enquirers focused inwards, on their own conscience to find the truth of metaphysical science. Ironically, despite the approach, the end result was the same— revelations led to the same conclusion of non-duality.'

'You'll have to help me understand how Einstein's revelation explains non-duality.'

'Well, Harry, when Einstein developed his famous formula of $E = mc^2$, he indicated that matter can be converted to energy that follows specific laws of physics. To explain in a layman's terms, let's take the Sun, for example. When millions of tonnes of hydrogen get converted to helium in the Sun, the chemical entity of hydrogen dies, giving rise to helium. This process produces an ethereal body, or sunlight, that can't be touched. But we can feel it in the form of light.

'These light waves travel millions of miles to arrive on Earth, pouring life into billions of trees, plants and seeds. Here, the intangible light becomes the physical entity called chlorophyll. Herbivores eat plants, and thrive and enrichen themselves. Carnivores eat herbivores. Thus, they are ultimately dependent on solar energy. Residual energy is stored in the trunks and stems of trees, only to reveal itself when those woods are placed in a fire. The cycle of hydrogen that begins on the Sun ends up on Earth in a multitude of life forms. Every molecule of energy produced is accounted for and recycled. Nothing is destroyed, but its manifestation is altered.

'Alternatively, we can say that energy manifests in the form of matter occasionally and then goes back to a form that we can feel but not see or touch.'

'So how do we apply this to life and death? How does this apply to our own selves?'

'Good question. And here is where I'll share my own learning curve. I chose to combine my learning and discovery of both the inward and the outward, both inside the physical body and outside it—a sort of melding of the Western and the Eastern approaches.

'I spent my formative years listening to my parents, and even monks who had explored their own deep subconscious existence to learn about life. Then, I learnt the physical sciences in school—physics, chemistry, biology, as well as the energy cycle. Out of my own curiosity, I studied ancient and modern philosophies while pursuing my medical training. So what I am today is a hybrid of my formative knowledge of modern sciences and my own inner quest.

'I have come to realize that at the peak of one's learning, all sciences converge on a common awareness of non-duality. My recent learning about the human genome and precision medicine, along with working with cancer patients every day, has given me an additional appreciation of the idea of organized life—from one cell to a complex human story.'

'Then how do you relate non-duality to life and death?'

'Let me bring in Watson and Crick's discovery of human chromosomes and genetics. By now, we have discovered that the blueprint of a physical body and life's engine is programmed by a complex genetic code hidden in the human genome. There are some very striking and startling findings. The human genome is almost three billion base pairs long, and the genetic code is universal. We only need 0.5 per cent, or somewhere around 50,000 genes, to exist as a human being.

'Our genome is a large blueprint and architectural drawing of complex formulas, combining molecules of proteins, fats and carbohydrates, facilitated by several signals and enzymes. We know that only 0.5 per cent of the blueprint is what we need to exist in this life. If someone were to change just 0.3 per cent, we'd be a different animal, not human any longer.

'Imagine that you have been granted the capacity to open up additional genes in your genome slowly, maybe one at a time. Perhaps your level of awareness will slowly rise. If only 0.5 per cent of the blueprint is enough to provide you with life as a human being, then imagine if all the secrets of the blueprint are revealed. Maybe the key to our mysteries lies there!'

Harry scooted to the edge of his chair. 'Wait. Are you implying that we can make an animal out of our genome?'

'Since the genetic code is universal, we can get any species. Think of a scenario where you have brick, mortar, wood and steel. Your master architect then asks you what you'd like to build. You could build a mansion. You could build a palace. You could build a skyscraper. The building blocks are all the same.

'Apart from our ancestral wisdom, non-duality has a base in science. When we understand the human genome and how it interacts with the broader nature around us, we can not only realize different avenues of learning but also modify our own genome as to who we are.'

'What? You mean we can modify our DNA?'

'Yes, indeed. New research reveals our capacity to send electric signals from neurons deep inside our genome through "epigenetic loci". These locations are communication channels that can stimulate newer genes, or alter existing genomic structures, to produce anti-inflammatory compounds. Research shows that one of the components of chromosome telomeres can be lengthened to increase our longevity.

'A group of scientists led by Dr Elissa Epel, a member of the National Academy of Medicine in the US, suggested that some types of meditation could lead to alterations in telomere length deep inside our genes and chromosomes at the microscopic level. And this could lead to longevity. Her team received the Nobel Prize for physiology in 2009. In another spectrum, a group of researchers at Harvard, under the leadership of Britta Holzel, revealed that there could be an increase in grey-matter density resulting from meditation. On the neurochemical front, practising mindfulness leads to signals altering the immune system in a favourable way. No matter what frontier of science we believe in, we have the tools to support, to a certain extent, the long-held belief in our own innate capacity to alter our own destiny.'

'Wow,' was all Harry could say.

'Let me bring us back to the outer world again. All our lives, our conditioning has limited our comprehension and interaction with the world outside us. I have already discussed the microscopic and macroscopic universe around us and how our limited vision has stunted our view of life in terms of measurable size. When we look at survivability, we can never fathom how life can exist at extreme temperatures. Now, we know that even inside volcanoes and geysers, thermophilic bacteria can survive and thrive at

120 degrees Centigrade. And deep under the ocean, life exists at extreme pressures.

'So the life that we do not see, the life that we do not think can exist, still exists outside our capacity of seeing, feeling, touching, hearing or smelling. The only way to expand our horizons to learn and enable our conscious understanding of the limitless scope of our existence is to tap into our own treasure trove of knowledge.'

'And how do we do that?' Harry asked.

'First, one needs to identify limitless awareness. What I call soul, what I define as the divine element within all of us, is that awareness. When we sleep, when we are distracted, when we are extroverted, that awareness is concealed or hidden. When we sleep, our eyes are there, our brain is there, our nervous system is still functioning, and yet, we do not see, do not feel, do not smell. So while all organ systems and the brain function are intact, along with all necessary neuronal wiring, there is one critical entity that is missing—awareness. That is our soul.

'Tapping into this deep subconscious, and seeking knowledge and understanding the mystery of life and death is where I have frequently chosen to seek refuge in times of dilemma and confusion. I am convinced that we indeed are a limitless and infinite existence, only limited by the scope of matter density. I do not see any discontinuity between myself and the rest of the universe. I have been a learner who has chosen to combine learning from both outside and inside of myself to come to an understanding that, for me, death is only a temporary stop in our journey to a much higher level of awareness. We are infinite, eternal beings that have chosen to be wrapped in this physical body for a temporary period. We are not human beings seeking divine experience. Rather, we are spiritual elements that experience this planet as humans. This is not the first time we are here, and this is not the last time we will be here. Maybe we have already existed in different life forms and shapes. In one form or another, I have been here in the universe.

'Harry, what you see today, in this body that you call Kashyap, may have previously been an ant, or a blade of grass, or a tree. My soul, or the genome, has chosen to select elements to wrap itself around, to take the shape and form that currently defines me. When my contract is over, I will return all of these elements to the earth, in whatever form my survivors choose to dispose me—and the soul or the divine element that inhabited this physical body will leave in the form of a wave, to merge into the all-pervading, self-existent, eternal, imperishable source of all things. Or, depending on my karma or desires left to be fulfilled, it will return to another life form and I will go through life once again.'

'How can you be sure of this genome changing into a wave form?'

'You can see the ice melting into water and water changing into vapour. But you don't see what happens to the vapour. It is still a residue of ice or water, but it has escaped your sight. Thus, upon death, you cannot see the soul leaving the physical body and becoming part of a larger ethereal space, but it still does occur.

'An iceberg dissolves in the ocean. Eventually, the ocean warms up and becomes vapour. That vapour eventually becomes a cloud. Someday, that cloud will burst, and come down again as rain, and eventually return to the ocean. Just as the human body dissolves and finds new forms in which to exist, the soul moves into a different destination of its own choice.

'So, for me, Harry, death is no different than an autumn leaf falling off a mature tree, dissolving into the soil below and coming back another spring. Life is eternal, continuous and indestructible. There may be metamorphoses and changes in form, shape and size in the space-time continuum, but it is still the same life force.'

'Then, doc, how can an agnostic like me liberate myself from these cycles of birth and death, over and over again?'

'Harry, I can summarize this way. I have learnt four paths to liberation. The first focuses on "karma yoga", the practice of selfless action and service. This path is almost identical to moral codes of conduct or commandments that every faith recommends as a way to live a good life.

'The second is "jnana yoga", the path of knowledge and wisdom. We have witnessed examples of this path since ages—from Aristotle to Ralph Waldo Emerson and Henry David Thoreau.

'The third path is "raja yoga", the meditative or contemplative practice. This is the path most commonly seen all over the world in the yoga of devotion and love for God.

'And the fourth is worship—the praising and praying to the god of your faith.

'Swami Vivekananda once said,

Each soul is potentially divine.
The goal is to manifest this divine within.
You can do this by work, worship, philosophy or meditation.
You can do this by one or all of these paths.

'We can look to one of the best-known scriptures of the Hindu tradition—the Bhagavad Gita, a text that comes from the great Hindu epic, the Mahabharata. In the text, Krishna, considered by his devotees to be the supreme god in human form, teaches the warrior Arjuna the truth of the eternal soul. Krishna assures Arjuna that if he kills his opponents on the battlefield, he kills only their bodies. The real self cannot be killed, so Arjuna need not mourn the dead.

'The Gita also discusses the possibility of liberation for the person who can let go of the ego to unite with the absolute. The individual self abides in the divine presence eternally, which in the Gita is understood as Krishna.'

Harry had heard enough for that day. He put his hands on his knees, as though preparing to rise from his chair, then paused.

'Doc,' he said, 'I want to die at home in my favourite bed. No matter what, I do not want to go to a hospital. I do not want a grand funeral. I want to be cremated in private and want my ashes to be dropped from a glider at the Soaring Club, where I taught flying.

'I will prepare and compose a letter to be sent out once my soul leaves my mortal body. I hope that my soul merges with a much larger omniscient, omnipotent divinity in the fourth dimension.

'I have no regrets, and now that you have helped me sort through my confusions and concerns, I am ready to take my flight into eternity. Bye, doc. I hope to catch up with you somewhere— either in the fourth dimension or maybe in another life form!'

I wasn't sure if the tears in his eyes were from the farewell or his pain—probably both.

I had to help Harry get up from his chair. Gingerly, we walked away from the dome. As we walked, Harry glanced back at everything, from dome to rooms to fountains and healing garden, knowing that he would never return.

13

The Flight to Eternity

And now I am eager to die into the deathless.
Into the audience-hall by the fathomless abyss where swells up
the music of toned strings I shall take the harp of my life.
I shall tune it to be the notes of forever, and when it has sobbed
out its last utterances, lay down my silent harp at the feet of
the silent.

—Rabindranath Tagore

On the day of Harry's farewell party, Susan felt a surreal blend
of joy and sadness—joy at having a party to honour Harry, and
sadness for the obvious reasons. Cancer had torn her life into two
parts—life before cancer, and life after the pathologist identified
cancer cells in Harry's liver and lungs.

But until the disease took Harry from her, she planned to
savour every word, every touch, every moment with him. She had
tried to weave the happy memories into a blanket of joy to keep
depression at bay. She had learnt that life allowed a finite number
of hugs, kisses and special moments. Too bad she hadn't realized
this important fact before Harry had got diagnosed with cancer.

As Susan completed the finishing touches to her hair, Harry stepped behind her. 'Well, how do I look?' he asked.

Susan turned and stepped back to take in the full effect of her husband. Her heart rate accelerated as her gaze travelled from the grey trousers to the white sweater to the navy blazer. He looked handsome. A sparkle from his lapel drew her attention.

'You're wearing your three-diamond pin,' she said as she buffed his cheek with a kiss.

'Tonight's special. Under the circumstances, I didn't think it was too showy.'

'I think it's perfect.'

'Just like my lovely wife,' he said, taking her arm.

Yes, he was special, and the three diamonds indicated his achievements as a flight instructor. Harry had earned the first diamond for gliding a distance of at least 500 kilometres, the second for flying at least 300 kilometres over an out-and-return or triangular course flown in the designated sequence. A party with his glider peers and students seemed a fitting send-off, and she wanted it to be special for him.

Susan was indexing each look, each smile, each phrase deep in her memory. 'Don't forget, never forget,' she silently chanted as she turned on to the dirt road that led to the Soaring Club. Although trees surrounded the 4,000-foot private airfield, the naked winter limbs no longer camouflaged their approach. She made a left turn on to Lift Lily Drive and drove the final distance to the clubhouse.

The main office and clubhouse were perfect for the party. The charming stone and vinyl structure had been designed and constructed for function as well as aesthetics. Adjacent to the airfield, it offered a perfect view of the landing strip. Tall windows lined one half of the building, and a porch lined the other half. Regardless of the weather, members could view take-offs, flights and landings from inside or outside. Tonight, George and Edith had decorated the interior viewing area for Harry and his guests.

Although Harry seldom complained, Susan had already witnessed the insidious effect of his disease in his diminished stamina, shortness of breath, weight loss and pallor. But not tonight. Tonight, Harry sparkled, in his element. He walked tall and proud as they crossed the porch where she had sat under the white ceiling fans and watched him land sailplanes so many times.

He stepped in as the man of the evening as easily as he stepped into his worn slippers. Brits didn't show off, but her Brit certainly made a fine showing. He joked and laughed and gave an eloquent speech challenging his young pilots to do more for gliding. By the end of the evening, Susan had fallen more deeply in love with the man she'd married—if that were even possible. Her feelings were bittersweet because they made her impending loss more difficult to accept. Too quickly, the party ended, and Susan brought home an exhausted but grateful husband.

Time, along with the cancer spreading through Harry's body, shifted to warp speed. As the tumour invaded his lung space, Harry had more difficulty breathing. The air was so precious that he spoke only in one- or two-word sentences until he received a call from Michael, one of his sons from whom he'd been estranged for more than twenty years.

Among Harry's deepest regrets in life were his three failed marriages and the resulting split with his sons. He had attempted to bridge the gap, but his sons had never accepted his calls, let alone his explanations.

Although Harry was sleeping when the phone rang, Susan didn't hesitate to awaken him.

'It's Michael,' she said as Harry opened his eyes.

She smiled at the sudden spark of interest in Harry's sunken features. Susan positioned him higher on the pillow and held the receiver for him. Although her heart ached for Harry as he struggled to breathe and speak to his son about his love and guilt for the time they hadn't shared, she whispered a 'thank you' for Harry's opportunity to make amends to Michael.

When Harry signalled the end of the conversation, Susan moved the receiver to her ear. 'Thanks for calling, Michael. Don't worry; I'll stay in touch.'

The conversation had drained the colour Michael's call had stimulated on Harry's face, but she could swear that one of the deep worry lines in his forehead had lessened. She kissed his cheek. Maybe the call had eased some of Harry's guilt and brought him peace.

The next day, I called Susan before visiting. 'Hi, Susan. How's he doing?'

'He's putting closure on the loose ends of his life. I'm scared . . . I don't want him to go,' she said, her voice breaking. 'I know how important these last few days are to him and that he doesn't want to leave anything unfinished before he leaves. But seeing him do it makes it all the more glaring that soon he won't be with us any more.'

'I know, Susan. He's been a wonderful husband and a great friend, and it's hard for me to let go too. But we still have the rest of our lives left. He doesn't. We need to be understanding now . . . put aside our selfish interest. God hasn't given us the ability to heal some diseases, but He has given us the chance to make our loved ones' last days on earth as meaningful and special as possible.'

I paused, my voice betraying that, as good as I was at giving this advice to patients' families, it was often difficult for me to follow my own counsel.

'I know, Kashyap. If you're available, please come by. He'd love to see you before . . . '

She couldn't finish her statement. She didn't have to.

'Of course. I'd love to.'

The next morning, I visited Harry's home and found him propped up in bed. His breathing was shallow, his face was hollow, but his smile lit up the room as I walked in and took his outstretched, emaciated hand.

'Harry. Still the charmer, huh?'

'You know it, doc. God blessed us Britishers with grace . . . and I'll be damned if I leave this world without it.'

He paused, as if unsure of how to continue. Then he drew as much breath as his lungs would allow and said, 'Doc, thank you for everything these past few months. Thank you for not fighting my wishes . . . about how I wanted to exit this world. Thank you for sharing your experiences with me to help me ease and plan my passing. You witnessed first-hand . . . the passing of a woman about to enter the prime of her life. Of a woman who fought every step of the way with such grace and bravery . . . despite continually being dealt the worst hands in life's game of poker. Of a woman whom we all thought had fought and won . . . and of her son who meant so much to you, and who was able . . . to erase his regrets before his passing.'

His words were frequently interrupted with coughs.

I patted his arm. 'Thanks for being part of my life, Harry. Your bravery, your smile and your grace have blessed us for as long as we've had the pleasure of knowing you.'

Susan left the room, unable to hold back her tears.

'Doc . . . will I pass away with grace?'

'Harry, all God has granted us is the ability to make the best of the hand we're dealt. You have lived your life to the fullest. You got to make your living doing what you love most every single day. Plenty of people who live decades longer never experience the satisfaction you got in one day alone. Now is the time to leave it in God's hands.'

My friend swallowed hard and seemed to relax a bit. 'Thank you, doc. I think this is time for goodbye. I wish I had more time to spend with Susan . . . and my children, and with friends such as you. But you're right. Like all the others you've told me about . . . it's almost time for me to let go. Goodbye, my friend. It's been an absolute pleasure. Thank you . . . for everything.'

I could only grasp his hand with both of mine, embrace him one last time, and leave before I broke down in response to his unbelievable strength and gratitude.

Harry continued deteriorating at such a frightening pace that Susan felt relief when Holly, Harry's daughter, arrived from England to help with his care.

'Hello, Dad,' Holly said.

'Engine checked and ready,' Harry whispered.

'What's this talk of airplanes?'

'Final destination,' Harry said.

As Harry declined, Susan and Holly sat on the bed with him and thumbed through photos of Harry's and Susan's life together. They passed stills of clear skies, red hawks, bald eagles and fluffy clouds merging and blurring together.

After closing the photo album, Susan cradled Harry's cool hand between her warm palms. 'What are you thinking?'

He gave her his signature smile. 'I want . . . a dignified exit.'

Susan blinked back tears. 'I'm your co-pilot, remember?'

'We've had . . . a grand flight. No grieving. Just good memories.'

'I'd do anything for you,' Susan said, 'but don't expect me not to miss you. I can't fulfil that promise.'

Harry gave her fingers a slight squeeze. 'Know what I want?'

Susan kissed his cheek. 'I'm afraid to ask.'

'Good soak. Wine. Music.'

'How about a nice sponge bath? You can relax right here in bed with your wine and music while I give you a bath and a good rubdown.'

He pushed up on his elbows. 'Tub. I can make it.'

'Holly and I will help you get there and back, but only if you wait until I get everything ready. And only if you promise you'll let me know if you don't think you have the strength.'

Harry's request terrified Susan. She would do anything for him. He asked for so little, and there was so little comfort she could offer. But a bath? What if he fell? What if they made it to the tub, but she and Holly couldn't get him out?

Her doubts and fears pestered her as she worked to make the bath perfect. She turned on Harry's favourite music, placed candles along the countertops, lit Harry's favourite incense and poured the wine. If Harry planned to exert the little bit of strength he possessed, then she'd do her best to create the ambience they'd shared on a very special night in the past.

Once Susan had prepared the bath, she approached his bed. Holly had left the room. Tidbit, Harry's cat, stood and stretched, but Harry's eyes remained closed. Adrenalin pumped through her veins as her gaze fell to his chest and waited for the barely perceptible rise of his breathing. The white linen rose as he tried to fill his failing lungs with air.

'Thank you,' she whispered, grateful that the end had not yet come. Then she asked aloud, 'Are you ready?'

'Patricia?' Harry asked as he rolled to his side. He was asking about his other daughter.

'She said she would let us know as soon as she could schedule a flight.'

Susan and Holly helped him to a sitting position on the side of the bed. 'Sit for a minute and give your body a chance to adjust,' Holly suggested.

Harry nodded as he struggled to fill his lungs with air. Susan fought the emotions welling up within her. His once-healthy frame was thin and frail beneath her fingers, the skin drooping over his skeleton. Then, aided by his wife and daughter, he stood and wobbled. He leaned heavily against Susan, but he'd lost so much weight that she was able to support him as they shuffled towards the bathroom. His once-confident, energetic stride had slowed to a nursing-home pace as he felt his way with long, bony toes.

Susan held her breath as he balanced on one foot to step into the tub, but he settled into the warm water without incident. The moment he leaned back against the rolled towel she had prepared as a headrest, her fear melted to joy. They'd done it. They'd performed a small task to give him pleasure.

Holly left to give them their privacy. Harry's face reddened from the exertion and the heat of the water. He gave Susan his famous smile—not the weak half-grin left by the disease, but the big toothy expression she'd witnessed the first time they'd met in Florida. She had fallen for him quickly, and it hadn't been just the way he had tutored her regarding glider flight. It was his calm self-assurance, the way he commanded himself and the situation, that sealed her admiration.

'Thank you,' he whispered as he accepted the glass she handed him.

Susan moved a chair close to the edge of the tub and held his hand in hers.

'Thank you,' she answered, her eyes filling with tears.

He sipped the wine with his eyes closed. 'Remember the night . . . I proposed?'

'I'll never forget.'

'Feels like . . . that night.'

Harry's dwindling strength allowed only a few minutes in the tub, but he seemed to enjoy every moment of it. In what seemed like the blink of an eye, Susan was gently patting his wasted flesh dry and helping him dress in clean bedclothes. She couldn't tell if the return walk was slower, but she could see the strain on his pursed lips and hear his grunts of exertion.

Midway to the bed, Harry stopped, leaned over slightly, and vomited.

As soon as she and Holly had him cleaned and comfortably back in bed, Susan called the hospice. Quickly, they delivered and administered medication for nausea and Harry's growing back pain. Now there was nothing to do but wait—a skill Susan had never successfully learnt.

Susan and Holly stayed close by. Susan savoured every opportunity to touch him, memorizing the feel of his hand in hers, of his brow beneath her fingertips. Separation was inevitable, but she had the time with him now, and she clung to each precious moment.

Although three cats shared the family home, Tidbit—the small calico—always remained close to Harry. Tidbit usually snuggled along his leg, but lately, restlessness had possessed the animal. Instead of snoozing the day away, he would sometimes jump up, leap from the bed, walk the inside perimeter of the house and return to the bed. But Tidbit wouldn't settle in one place for long.

When Tidbit stretched and jumped from the bed the fourth time, Harry's eyes opened. He pointed to his daughter Patricia's photograph on the bedside table.

Susan understood. 'I'll call her.'

Through the overseas line, Patricia's voice sounded distant. 'I got an early flight. I should be there day after tomorrow.'

Susan covered the receiver. 'She got a flight.'

Harry nodded.

'Tell Dad I love him. If he has to leave early, I'll understand.'

When Susan signed off with Patricia, she turned to find Harry watching her intently. 'Stay strong for him,' she told herself. 'Patricia says it's okay if you need to leave. She loves you.'

Relief came over his gaunt features. He closed his eyes and breathed a little deeper, then opened his eyes and searched

Susan's face. It was as if he had spoken a query. Harry needed to know she would be all right after his death. Although certain of her next action, she needed a few moments to compose herself.

Tidbit returned to the bed, but their other two cats, an orange tabby and a grey striped one, continued to prowl in the hall. Susan left the room to collect the two malingerers. After a few moments, she returned and released the cats on to the bed and sat down beside Harry. Her heart ached at how the ravages of the disease had robbed him of his health and how hard he struggled to maintain his dignity. Worse, most of his struggle was for those he loved most.

She wrapped her right arm around Harry's neck and slowly whispered, 'It's okay to leave. I'm going to be fine.'

'We will miss you, Dad, but we will be okay,' Holly agreed gently.

For the first time in days, a sense of calm came over him. As if in agreement, the cats also relaxed and nestled at his side.

In a few hours, Harry slipped into a coma. Cancer had forced him to accept his fate, but Susan struggled with releasing the man she loved so dearly. During her career, she had dealt with adverse situations, particularly patients diagnosed with cancer. She thought she was strong; she thought she had come to grips with the disease and with death. Yes, she had an exterior strength honed to assist patients, but on the inside—on the inside, she was fragile. Harry was her strength. He had accepted his approaching death with calm composure.

Two days later, on a glorious sunny morning, Susan was seated on the bed on one side of Harry. Holly was in the chair on the other side of the bed. Between them, Harry's breathing had slowed, signalling that his coma had deepened. His breathing became chaotic and irregular, with just three or four shallow breaths per minute. It looked like he was trying to open his eyes, perhaps to view the distant skies one last time.

Susan pressed the back of her fingers against his cheek. 'It's okay, honey. Patricia is coming. Her flight is probably somewhere over the Atlantic, but you don't have to wait. Remember, she sent her love and her permission for you to go.'

Harry's body jerked a bit. His eyes remained closed, but his arms stretched out as if he were trying to embrace something in the air. His facial features softened. His tense eyebrows relaxed. Susan straightened the linen, but Harry and the cats continued to sleep.

Suddenly, Tidbit leapt from the bed and raced to the family room. The cat's exit was followed by sounds of furniture banging against the floor.

'What's that all about?' Holly asked.

Susan stood. 'I don't know. Maybe there's a dog outside.'

Together, they retraced Tidbit's wild flight from the bedroom to the family room. Although they found the results of his movements, they didn't find Tidbit or the source of his erratic behaviour. Still baffled, they returned to the bedroom.

At that moment, the realization was instantaneous. Tidbit had granted Harry's last request. With dignity and privacy, Harry had exited his body like a discarded pair of worn khakis and started his journey to the next life.

Susan swallowed to help push words past her bone-dry throat. 'He's gone.'

Holly stiffened. 'How can you know?'

How could she know? Susan stroked Harry's cool cheek. This time, the emptiness she felt threatened to drown her in sorrow.

Susan struggled for control. 'We need to call the funeral home. He wouldn't want anyone to come to view his body.'

From that moment on, time passed in blinks.

The hearse arrived. Numb, Susan and Holly waited as the attendants gently placed Harry's body on the gurney and wheeled him outside, away from their house for the final time.

One of the attendants pushed the hearse door closed. It failed. He pushed again.

A bubble of laughter escaped Susan's throat, followed by one from Holly. 'We'd better follow them in case they drop him out the back, and we need to pick him up,' Susan said.

Holly's laughter increased and, although an incredible sadness overwhelmed them, they hugged and laughed and cried as they closed the door.

In his last conversations with her, Harry had referred to his death as his final journey. He wasn't the only one who had begun a new journey. How could she live without Harry at her side? For weeks, she'd lived with the knowledge that he would leave, but she hadn't believed it. She still couldn't believe it. Maybe that was the source of this fog in her mind. She was living in a cloud of grief.

The folder with Harry's final instructions loomed over her. She wasn't going to open it because if she read the instructions, she would be accepting his departure. What would happen if she didn't go forward? What if she were to play mind games to try to keep Harry's presence near her?

Patricia arrived from Great Britain. The funeral home called to ask if Susan, Holly and Patricia would want to attend Harry's cremation.

Susan turned to Holly. 'Would you like to come?'

Holly shook her head. 'No. I want to remember him as he lived, not . . . ' her voice faded.

'Patricia?' Susan asked.

Patricia nodded.

On the drive to the crematorium, Patricia said, 'I felt him say goodbye the moment he died, you know.'

Susan's mind scrambled to interpret Patricia's statement. 'I'm sorry, what did you say?'

'Dad died at noon?'

'Yes,' Susan said.

'My flight was above the Atlantic. I felt him around me, and I knew he needed to go, so I prayed. It was glorious. I felt the angels lift Dad into their palms. He's at peace, Susan—truly at peace.'

Patricia's words swirled in Susan's mind until they walked arm in arm to the crematorium entrance. 'Thank you for telling me about your vision about Harry,' she said.

Patricia stopped with her hand on the door. 'It's one of the memories that help me. I hope it helps you too. Are you ready to go in?'

Susan wanted to scream no. But she couldn't stop the cremation any more than she could stop the cancer from taking Harry's life. Although Susan wanted to keep Harry near her forever, Patricia's confession had eased her own immediate pain. Harry was at peace and had died on his own terms. Susan held this thought close, clinging to the small comfort it offered.

George, their close friend and owner of the gliding centre, demonstrated his love and respect for Harry by releasing Harry's ashes over the airfield. Susan wondered how many test flights George had made to ensure the perfect release. She knew that if Harry were watching, he would have a big, toothy grin on his face. She squeezed her eyes tightly closed, sharpening Harry's image in her mind.

'I think you should have this.'

Susan swallowed past the lump in her throat. How had she gotten from the airfield to the parking lot? When had the service ended? Beside her, a member of the Gliding Club held out a piece of paper.

He gave her a reassuring smile as if he understood her struggle. 'I couldn't believe it,' he said. 'Every pilot here has tried and failed to hit the X. This landed on it precisely.'

Susan accepted the paper bag that had held Harry's ashes. It was as if she didn't feel the bag in her hands.

What was the member's name? She knew him, but names and faces seemed to blur into the haze she was in. Without speaking, he moulded his hands around hers, squeezed, then left. A reassuring thought formed as Susan rubbed her fingers across the surface of the paper. Harry had arrived at his new destination and was okay.

Like Harry, she had a new destination in front of her. Healing would take a long time, but someday, she was going to be okay too.

Epilogue
Concluding My Journey

My journey to self-discovery began almost fifty years ago when, as an eight-year-old child, I went to watch a feature film in Hindi with my parents. The movie was called *Anand*. It was a tragic story, in which the main character, Raja Babu, dies of cancer.

I was inconsolable at the death. For several days, I cried. Finally, my dad suggested that when I grow up, I become a doctor and help people like Raja Babu.

As a young adult, I bought a red motorcycle and started riding around rural India in search of the beauty of nature, tranquillity and serenity. With a camera slung across my shoulder and a dilapidated satchel across my back, I zoomed through villages and across jungles teeming with wildlife. As lions roared and birds sang, and villagers fed their cows, I was searching for that 'One' that would give me lasting bliss and peace. I struggled to find myself and my calling in this life.

These journeys of reflection and self-discovery brought me across the seven seas. I never realized that the answer to who I was, where I came from, and where I will spend eternity was always within me. That what I was looking for was, is and will always be there, an inseparable part of me.

I have always been part of the universe. Even before I was born, I was floating in the universe like a brown autumn leaf, freely, as part of the cosmic consciousness. Then I decided to experience human life for a limited span, as my genome-encoded DNA mixed a blueprint of this body with elements borrowed from the planet Earth. Now people call this part of the cosmic consciousness 'Kashyap'.

But through all of my searching, I never forgot my dad's encouragement to become a doctor. Now, as an oncologist living with life and death every day, I have come to a realization that I am nothing but an awareness covered in a temporary shelter of a physical body that Mother Nature granted from the basic elements of life.

In these few episodes of learning from other enquirers like me, I have shared their journeys through their physical bodies and then back into the higher awareness or wherever they chose to move on to. Harry has granted linguistic tone to my understanding of life and death. I have shared my quest from ignorance to bliss, from darkness to light, and one day, I will start my own transcendence from death of this physical body to immortal soul.

I invite you to join in my journey as we explore this eternal cycle of love and bliss around us. We can find that light even in the darkest hour of death. If you find yourself watching this play of life and death all around us, yet notice eternal bliss and light amid it all, and live life to the fullest as if there is no tomorrow, I feel my efforts will have been paid.